Presented to:

Michelle

BY:

Mrs. Hess

Date:

February,
2005

11/11

extreme for Jesus

promise book

RON LUCE

J. COUNTRYMAN
Nashville, TN

Published by J. Countryman®, a division of Thomas Nelson,
Inc., Nashville, Tennessee 37214

All Scripture quotations in this book are from
the New King James Version of the Bible (NKJV),
copyright © 1979, 1980, 1982, Thomas Nelson, Inc., Publishers.

J. Countryman® is a trademark of Thomas Nelson, Inc.

Project editor: Jenny Baumgartner

Designed by Uttley/DouPonce DesignWorks
Sisters, Oregon

Published in association with the literary agency of
Alive Communications, 1465 Kelly Johnson Blvd., Suite 320,
Colorado Springs, Colorado 80920

Teen Mania Ministries
P.O Box 2000, Garden Valley, TX 75771, 1-800-299-TEEN
www.acquirethefire.com or www.teenmania.org

ISBN 0-8499-5606-4

Printed and bound in Belgium

www.jcountryman.com

So you have a desire to be **extreme for Jesus Christ**—that's awesome! There are thousands of other young people just like you, rising up all over America and around the world. They are part of a new generation of believers who refuse to compromise and want to stand strong for God.

This book will help you keep the fire going, even when troubles hit your life. In these pages, you'll find Scripture-based advice for over eighty different issues, with applicable Bible verses on the opposite page. I encourage you to begin reading now, even *before* you meet a challenge. Keep this book with your Bible and next to your bed so that it will be handy whenever you need it.

You don't ever have to lose your fire for God. This book will give you the spiritual food you need for overcoming anything the devil or the world might throw at you.

God bless you as you continue to be extreme and change this world for Jesus Christ.

RON LUCE

Table of Contents

Extreme

Promises

Of

Be strong and of good courage, do not fear nor be afraid of them; for the Lord your God, He is the One who goes with you. He will not leave you nor forsake you.

—Deuteronomy 31:6

When my father and my mother forsake me, then the Lord will take care of me.

—Psalm 27:10

Fear not, for I am with you;
Be not dismayed, for I am your God.
I will strengthen you,
Yes, I will help you,
I will uphold you with My righteous right hand.

—Isaiah 41:10

For I am persuaded that neither death nor life, nor angels nor principalities nor powers, nor things present nor things to come, nor height nor depth, nor any other created thing, shall be able to separate us from the love of God which is in Christ Jesus our Lord.

—Romans 8:38–39

WHAT TO DO
When You Are
Lonely

Jesus knew what it felt like to be alone. He was nailed to the cross when all of humanity had turned their back on Him. Even His Father had to turn His back because God couldn't look at our sin. **Jesus knows** exactly how you feel.

It is easy to feel lonely in this fast-paced, high-tech world. So much of our time is spent with high-tech toys—Discmans, computers, video games, VCRs—that we forget to spend time with people. We busy ourselves with *things,* but we feel absolutely isolated. As a result, our time is filled, but our hearts are empty. If you feel lonely, then try turning off your toys, and try reaching out to people.

The Bible says, "A man who has friends must himself be friendly" (Prov. 18:24). Reach out and befriend somebody. Try **sharing your heart** a little bit. Above all, remember Philippians 4:19: "My God shall supply all your need." He knows your need for friendships. Ask Him to fill that lonely part of your heart.

Lord, I ask you to meet my needs. I ask you to bring the right kinds of friends to me that will be used by you to fill my longing for deep relationships. In Jesus' name. Amen.

You will keep him in perfect peace,
Whose mind is stayed on You,
Because he trusts in You.
Trust in the Lord forever,
For in Yah, the Lord, is everlasting strength.

—ISAIAH 26:3–4

Therefore do not worry, saying, 'What shall we eat?' or 'What shall we drink?' or 'What shall we wear?' For after all these things the Gentiles seek. For your heavenly Father knows that you need all these things. But seek first the kingdom of God and His righteousness, and all these things shall be added to you. Therefore do not worry about tomorrow, for tomorrow will worry about its own things. Sufficient for the day is its own trouble.

—MATTHEW 6:31–34

Peace, I leave with you, My peace I give to you; not as the world gives do I give to you. Let not your heart be troubled, neither let it be afraid.

—JOHN 14:27

Cast all your care upon Him, for He cares for you.

—1 PETER 5:7

WHAT TO DO
When You Are
Worried

Since the beginning of time, humans have been prone to worry. Back in the New Testament times, Jesus had to remind people, "Do not worry, saying, 'What shall we eat?' or 'What shall we drink?' or 'What shall we wear?'" (Matt 6:31).

It is so easy to get **caught up** with the rest of the world, worrying about life. *Will I pass my test? Are people going to like me? Will my family stay together? What kind of job will I have in the future?* These concerns are real, but Jesus did not say, "Just pretend that they are not there." Instead, He asks us to *choose* what we will dwell on. Will you hold on to your cares and worries, or will you lay them down before God?

As a Christian, you do not have to worry because you have an incredible Father who cares more about you than you can possibly imagine. So **seek Him first**, and let Him take care of you.

Lord Jesus, today I give you my worries and fears about the future. I choose to seek you first. I know that you will take care of every part of my life. In your name. Amen.

He heals the brokenhearted
And binds up their wounds.

—PSALM 147:3

But those who wait on the Lord
Shall renew their strength;
They shall mount up with wings like eagles,
They shall run and not be weary,
They shall walk and not faint.

—ISAIAH 40:31

Blessed be the God and Father of our Lord Jesus Christ, the Father of mercies and God of all comfort, who comforts us in our tribulation, that we may be able to comfort those who are in any trouble, with the comfort with which we ourselves are comforted by God.

—2 CORINTHIANS 1:3–4

Beloved, do not think it strange concerning the fiery trial which is to try you, as though some strange thing happened to you; but rejoice to the extent that you partake of Christ's sufferings, that when His glory is revealed, you may also be glad with exceeding joy.

—1 PETER 4:12–13

WHAT TO DO
When You Are
Depressed

If you have turned here today, it is probably because someone or something has really let you down.

Remember David? He also had a depressing experience. After killing the giant, David presumed that he had earned great favor with the king, but all of a sudden, King Saul began to throw spears at him. David ran for his life, and eventually, he had to act like a madman so that the soldiers wouldn't kill him. David had a lot of reasons to be discouraged, but what was his response? In Psalm 42:5, he says, "Why are you cast down, O my soul? . . . Hope in God."

In other words, in the middle of being totally discouraged, he says, "Why am I depressed? I **choose** to put my hope in God! I refuse to be overwhelmed by my circumstances. I will put my confidence in my God. He will lift me up, and He will take care of me and protect me."

Lord, despite what has happened to me, I will put my hope in you. I believe that you will work out all things for good. In Jesus' name. Amen.

I acknowledged my sin to you,
And my iniquity I have not hidden.
I said, "I will confess my transgressions to the
    Lord,"
And you forgave the iniquity of my sin.

—Psalm 32:5

For God did not send His Son into the world to condemn the world, but that the world through Him might be saved. He who believes in Him is not condemned; but he who does not believe is condemned already, because he has not believed in the name of the only begotten Son of God.

—John 3:17–18

If we confess our sins, He is faithful and just to forgive us our sins and to cleanse us from all unrighteousness.

—1 John 1:9

Then I heard a loud voice saying in heaven, "Now salvation, and strength, and the kingdom of God, and the power of His Christ have come, for the accuser of our brethren, who accused them before our God day and night, has been cast down."

—Revelation 12:10

WHAT TO DO
When You Are
Guilty

You've probably turned to this page because you've just blown it, really bad. If that's true, then you're probably feeling frustrated and angry at yourself.

Right now is a very **critical moment** for you because if you keep beating yourself up, then you could push yourself away from God. But God knew what you were going to do even before you did it, and He loves you all the same!

Remember that Satan is "the accuser of our brethren" (Rev. 12:10). In other words, Satan is pointing the finger at you, making you feel lousy and rubbing your face in the dirt. He wants to make you feel so bad that you won't come back to God and ask for forgiveness.

How do you deal with guilt? The Bible says if we confess our sins, God is faithful and just to forgive us (1 John 1:9). Don't try to justify your behavior; it's no one else's fault. Confess it. Humbly come to the Lord, and He will forgive you.

Lord, I come to you and confess my sin. I blew it. I am sorry. I repent. Thank you for cleansing me and purifying my heart once again. In Jesus' name. Amen.

I will instruct you and teach you in the way
you should go;
I will guide you with My eye.

—Psalm 32:8

Trust in the Lord with all your heart,
And lean not on your own understanding;
In all your ways acknowledge Him,
And He shall direct your paths.

—Proverbs 3:5–6

God is not the author of confusion but of
peace.

—1 Corinthians 14:33

For where envy and self-seeking exist, confusion and every evil thing are there. But the
wisdom that is from above is first pure, then
peaceable, gentle, willing to yield, full of mercy
and good fruits, without partiality and without
hypocrisy. Now the fruit of righteousness is sown
in peace by those who make peace.

—James 3:16–18

WHAT TO DO
When You Are Confused

The Bible says that God is not the author of confusion (1 Cor. 14:33). So, where is your confusion coming from? What about the people you are hanging out with? The movies you've been watching? The music you are listening to?

You can get rid of the confusion! Do away with those things that contradict God's Word. Don't let confusion into your brain or heart. Continuing to let it in is like intentionally adding static to your TV so that you can't really see the picture. Or putting a slow modem on your computer so that you can't see or hear the information you want.

Identify the **source** of your confusion, and refuse to allow it into your life! Hang on to what you know is true about God and His Word.

Lord Jesus, I rebuke this spirit of confusion that has tried to attack me. I refuse to continue watching or listening to things that bring this confusion into my life. In your name. Amen.

Your word I have hidden in my heart,
That I might not sin against You.

—Psalm 119:11

He will not allow you to be tempted beyond what you are able, but with the temptation will also make the way of escape, that you may be able to bear it.

—1 Corinthians 10:13

Put on the whole armor of God, that you may be able to stand against the wiles of the devil. . . . the sword of the Spirit, which is the word of God.

—Ephesians 6:11, 17

We do not have a High Priest who cannot sympathize with our weaknesses, but was in all points tempted as we are, yet without sin. Let us therefore come boldly to the throne of grace, that we may obtain mercy and find grace to help in time of need.

—Hebrews 4:15–16

Let no one say when he is tempted, "I am tempted by God"; for God cannot be tempted by evil, nor does He Himself tempt anyone. But each one is tempted when he is drawn away by his own desires and enticed.

—James 1:13–14

WHAT TO DO
When You Are Tempted

It is very important that you prepare for temptation even *before* you are tempted. **Right now**, you need to get strong in the areas where you are weak. To become stronger, you need to "work out" your faith, much like going to a gym. You have to "pump" the Word of God into your heart to build "muscles" of faith.

Some people fall into the same temptation again and again because they have not "exercised" with the Word. As a result, their faith is weak, and they become easy prey for the enemy.

If you go to the gym and *watch* other people work out, you won't get any stronger. In the same way, you can't get to know the Word by watching your pastor or youth pastor study and memorize the verses. You have to do it for yourself. Then you can respond like Jesus did when he was tempted: He said to the enemy, "It is written . . ." (Matt. 4:4, 7, 10).

Lord Jesus, I commit to pumping your Word into my heart, especially in those areas where I am tempted the most. Then I will be strong when temptation comes my way. In your name. Amen.

Rest in the Lord, and wait patiently for Him;
Do not fret because of him who prospers in his
way,
Because of the man who brings wicked
schemes to pass.
Cease from anger, and forsake wrath;
Do not fret—it only causes harm.

—Psalm 37:7–8

A soft answer turns away wrath,
but a harsh word stirs up anger.

—Proverbs 15:1

Let all bitterness, wrath, anger, clamor, and
evil speaking be put away from you, with all
malice. And be kind to one another, tenderhearted,
forgiving one another, just as God in Christ forgave you.

—Ephesians 4:31–32

My beloved brethren, let every man be swift to
hear, slow to speak, slow to wrath; for the wrath
of man does not produce the righteousness of God.

—James 1:19–20

WHAT TO DO
When You Are
Angry

The Bible says: "Be angry, and do not sin" (Eph. 4:26). It's okay to feel angry, but don't become so angry that you sin, that you treat people like garbage. That same verse also says, "Do not let the sun go down on your wrath." If you are angry, do not stay angry even for one day.

God asks us to forgive others just as He has forgiven us. That is how you deal with anger: you let it go. You choose to forgive, even if you don't think the person deserves it, even if you don't want to forgive, and even if they haven't asked you to forgive them. If you hold anger in your heart, it is just like cancer—it can infect your entire personality. If you are angry today, choose to forgive before the sun goes down tonight.

Lord Jesus, I thank you that because you forgave me, I can forgive others. I choose to do that now, and with your power, I can. In your name. Amen.

For the LORD does not see as man sees; for man looks at the outward appearance, but the LORD looks at the heart.

—1 SAMUEL 16:7

The LORD is near to those who have a broken
    heart,
and saves such as have a contrite spirit.

—PSALM 34:18

Commit to the LORD,
Trust also in Him,
And He shall bring it to pass.

—PSALM 37:5

Therefore, as the elect of God, holy and beloved, put on tender mercies, kindness, humility, meekness, longsuffering; bearing with one another, and forgiving one another, if anyone has a complaint against another; even as Christ forgave you, so you also must do. But above all these things put on love, which is the bond of perfection.

—COLOSSIANS 3:12–14

WHAT TO DO
When You Are Rejected

Did you know that rejection has less to do with *you* and more to do with *those rejecting?* People have a **battle** going on inside themselves between their flesh and spirit. When the flesh takes over, people begin to put others down so that they will feel more superior. The more they put others down, the better they think they are. It's about their insecurity and not about your worth.

Jesus knows how you feel. The Scripture says that Jesus was "despised and rejected by men" (Isa. 53:3), but Jesus knew He was loved by His Father. You can be sure that no matter what people say about you, you are not rejected by God—you are **accepted** by Him. Find your security in His love and not in other people's opinions about you.

Lord, I thank you that no matter what people say about me or how they treat me, you accept me and you love me just the way I am. I refuse to let them dictate my worth and my importance. In Jesus' name. Amen.

For rebellion is as the sin of witchcraft, and stubbornness is as iniquity and idolatry.

—1 SAMUEL 15:23

A wise man fears and departs from evil,
But a fool rages and is self-confident.
A quick-tempered man acts foolishly,
And a man of wicked intentions is hated.

—PROVERBS 14:16–17

Obey those who rule over you, and be submissive, for they watch out for your souls, as those who must give account. Let them do so with joy and not with grief, for that would be unprofitable for you.

—HEBREWS 13:17

Likewise you younger people, submit yourselves to your elders. Yes, all of you be submissive to one another, and be clothed with humility, for
"God resists the proud,
But gives grace to the humble."

—1 PETER 5:5

WHAT TO DO
When You Are
Rebellious

For the rest of our lives, we are all going to be under some kind of authority—a teacher, boss, pastor, police officer, and so on. Did you know that God's blessings on your life occur in **direct proportion** to your response to authority? If you have a humble and submissive attitude toward your leaders, then God will bless your life. On the other hand, if you manipulate others and try to get your own way, then you will get stung in the process. Remember that when Satan rebelled against God, he was cast out of heaven.

The Bible says rebellion is "the sin of witchcraft" (1 Sam. 15:23). When you rebel against authority, you are acting like the devil. Choose now to have a humble attitude toward authority, and God will bless you.

Lord, please forgive my stubborn, rebellious attitude. I choose to humble myself and have a submissive attitude toward all the leaders and authorities in my life, and I thank you that your blessings will cover me as a result. In Jesus' name. Amen.

Extreme Promises

Promises

for

Your Personal Relationships

If there is among you a poor man of your brethren, within any of the gates in your land which the Lord your God is giving you, you shall not harden your heart nor shut your hand from your poor brother, but you shall open your hand wide to him and willingly lend him sufficient for his need, whatever he needs.

—DEUTERONOMY 15:7–8

Pure and undefiled religion before God and the Father is this: to visit orphans and widows in their trouble, and to keep oneself unspotted from the world.

—JAMES 1:27

If a brother or sister is naked and destitute of daily food, and one of you says to them, "Depart in peace, be warmed and filled," but you do not give them the things which are needed for the body, what does it profit?

—JAMES 2:15–16

HOW TO
Serve Others

Do you live to *give* or do you live to *get*? Most people in our society live to **get**. They want to get attention, approval, or admiration. They live a very "me-centered" life. They are so busy thinking about themselves that they don't have time to think about anyone else.

But Jesus lived His life to *give*. He encourages us to give our lives away in the same way that He did. You can choose to be either a giver or a getter. Look for opportunities to give love, compassion, money, or kindness. Live to give your life away and serve others. Jesus said, "Whoever desires to become great among you, let him be your servant" (Matt. 20:26). An anonymous quote also puts it this way: "Be kinder than people deserve because they probably need it more than you know."

Lord, I refuse to be like the rest of the world in being "me-centered." Today I choose to live my life to give it away so that I can touch others. In Jesus' name. Amen.

But I say to you, love your enemies, bless those who curse you, do good to those who hate you, and pray for those who spitefully use you and persecute you.

—Matthew 5:44

For if you forgive men their trespasses, your heavenly Father will also forgive you. But if you do not forgive men their trespasses, neither will your Father forgive your trespasses.

—Matthew 6:14–15

And whenever you stand praying, if you have anything against anyone, forgive him, that your Father in heaven may also forgive you your trespasses.

—Mark 11:25

Not returning evil for evil or reviling for reviling, but on the contrary blessing, knowing that you were called to this, that you may inherit a blessing. For

"He who would love life
And see good days,
Let him refrain his tongue from evil,
And his lips from speaking deceit."

—1 Peter 3:9–10

HOW TO
Forgive Others

Forgiving others is a **decision,** not a feeling. If we waited until we felt like forgiving, then none of us would ever forgive anybody. When someone has hurt us, our first thought is, *They don't deserve forgiveness.* Well, of course they don't. The fact is neither do we. We didn't deserve Jesus' sacrifice of dying on the cross for us, but He did it—and He gave us *His* forgiveness.

Remember the parable about the master who forgave his servant's huge debt? That same servant then refused to forgive a debt that another man owed him and put him in jail. When the master heard this, he then refused to forgive his servant's huge debt (Matt. 18:21–35).

Jesus' point is that the amount of forgiveness you give is the same amount of grace and forgiveness you will receive. If you are a shrewd judge and you refuse to let go of people's wrongs toward you, then you will never feel the freedom of forgiveness that Jesus offers for the wrongs you do to Him.

Lord, I choose to forgive. I am making this decision right now, even though I may not feel like it. In Jesus' name. Amen.

31

And whoever gives one of these little ones only a cup of cold water in the name of a disciple, assuredly, I say to you, he shall by no means lose his reward.

—MATTHEW 10:42

So the people asked him, saying, "What shall we do then?" He answered and said to them, "He who has two tunics, let him give to him who has none; and he who has food, let him do likewise."

—LUKE 3:10–11

No longer do I call you servants, for a servant does not know what his master is doing; but I have called you friends, for all things that I heard from My Father I have made known to you.

—JOHN 15:15

By this we know love, because He laid down His life for us. And we also ought to lay down our lives for the brethren. But whoever has this world's goods, and sees his brother in need, and shuts up his heart from him, how does the love of God abide in him? My little children, let us not love in word or in tongue, but in deed and in truth.

—1 JOHN 3:16–18

HOW TO
Be a Better Friend

In John 15:15, Jesus says to His disciples: "I have called you friends, for all things that I heard from My Father I have made known to you." In this verse, Jesus is explaining the depth of His feelings. He was basically saying, "You guys aren't acquaintances. You are my **friends.** You know more than what's in my head. You know the deepest things in my heart, those things My Father has shared with me, and I have shared them with you."

People today have many acquaintances but hardly any deep friendships. The way to a deeper level of true friendship is to really begin sharing a part of your **heart,** the deepest part of you, with someone else. Instead of waiting for a great friendship to just happen, begin to share what you are thinking and feeling. Then watch how other people respond. Not all of them—but some of them—will soon begin to share *their* heart with you.

Lord, I thank you that I don't have to go through my life with just a bunch of acquaintances. Thank you for bringing deep friendships into my life that will challenge me and help me to grow in you. In Jesus' name. Amen.

Again I say to you that if two of you agree on earth concerning anything that they ask, it will be done for them by My Father in heaven. For where two or three are gathered together in My name, I am there in the midst of them.

—MATTHEW 18:19–20

But I say to you who hear: Love your enemies, do good to those who hate you, bless those who curse you, and pray for those who spitefully use you.

—LUKE 6:27–28

Now I beg you, brethren, through the Lord Jesus Christ, and through the love of the Spirit, that you strive together with me in prayers to God for me.

—ROMANS 15:30

Confess your trespasses to one another, and pray for one another, that you may be healed. The effective, fervent prayer of a righteous man avails much.

—JAMES 5:16

HOW TO
Pray for Others

One of the best ways to care about other people is to really pray for them. Not just in a casual way, but really praying about their families, their lives, and what they are thinking and feeling. Praying for others is a **selfless** gesture that causes you to love them on a whole different level. They will feel a depth of compassion about you, something that tells them that you really care for them—because you care for them on your knees.

When you pray for others, you begin to see them the way God sees them. And when that happens, you begin to love them with His love. The fact is, Jesus loves them way more than you ever could. If you're praying for your friends and family to go to heaven with you, remember that God wants them in heaven also—but not just because *you* want them there, but because Jesus died on the cross to save them. That's the **deepest love** possible. Pray for others with His love.

Lord Jesus, open my eyes to see my friends and family with your eyes and to care for them and treat them the way that you do. In your name. Amen.

Blessed are the peacemakers,
For they shall be called sons of God.

—MATTHEW 5:9

For I say, through the grace given to me, to everyone who is among you, not to think of himself more highly than he ought to think, but to think soberly, as God has dealt to each one a measure of faith.

—ROMANS 12:3

Repay no one evil for evil. Have regard for good things in the sight of all men. If it is possible, as much as depends on you, live peaceably with all men. . . . Do not be overcome by evil, but overcome evil with good.

—ROMANS 12:17–18, 21

Become complete. Be of good comfort, be of one mind, live in peace; and the God of love and peace will be with you.

—2 CORINTHIANS 13:11

HOW TO

Cope with Conflict

What is your first response when someone disagrees with you? A person with an untamed character will respond the way most people do: by flying off the handle. The Bible gives us a prescription for what to do when two people disagree. It says to give "preference to one another" (Rom. 12:10). In other words, we don't always have to be right, and we shouldn't always have to get our way. Instead, God asks us to seek the best for one another. He wants us to put others before ourselves.

The psalmist says he restrained his tongue even while his heart was "hot within" him (Ps. 39:1, 3). You don't have to let disagreements push your buttons. You can control your response. What others do or say to you doesn't have to determine your behavior. Having a humble heart and refining your character will make you respond more like Jesus would.

Lord, I refuse to let others push my buttons today. I choose to prefer others over myself, rather than trying to get my own way. In Jesus' name. Amen.

The thoughts of the wicked are an abomina-
tion to the Lord,
But the words of the pure are pleasant.

—PROVERBS 15:26

He who covers a transgression seeks love,
But he who repeats a matter separates
friends.

—PROVERBS 17:9

But why do you judge your brother? Or why do
you show contempt for your brother? For we shall
all stand before the judgment seat of Christ.

—ROMANS 14:10

Finally, all of you be of one mind, having
compassion for one another; love as brothers, be
tenderhearted, be courteous; not returning evil
for evil or reviling for reviling, but on the contrary blessing, knowing that you were called to
this, that you may inherit a blessing.

—1 PETER 3:8–9

HOW TO
Resolve
Resentment

Resentment begins when we fail to forgive. Maybe you tried to forgive somebody, but then that person kept doing the same thing to you over and over again. Maybe it was a certain circumstance that happened to you—maybe you were violently abused, and you don't feel like you could ever forgive. But the longer you refuse to forgive, the more it turns into bitterness, and that bitterness will stain your heart and affect every part of your personality.

If you think that you can hurt those who hurt you by being bitter and resentful toward them, you are really only hurting yourself. If your bitterness stems from a recurring situation, then I encourage you to do this: forgive them *in advance.* If you recognize that they are human, then your attitude will be, "I thought this might happen, but I have already forgiven them."

Lord, I thank you that you do not resent me even though I do a lot of things that could cause you to resent me. I choose to forgive those who have hurt me in the past so that if they hurt me again, I will hold no bitterness in my heart. In Jesus' name. Amen.

Honor your father and your mother, that your days may be long upon the land which the LORD your God is giving you.

—EXODUS 20:12

Honor your father and your mother, as the LORD your God has commanded you, that your days may be long, and that it may be well with you in the land which the LORD your God is giving you.

—DEUTERONOMY 5:16

Children, obey your parents in the Lord, for this is right. "Honor your father and mother," which is the first commandment.

—EPHESIANS 6:1–2

HOW TO

Develop a Relationship with Your Parents

Along with love, parents want these two things from their children: obedience and honor. When your mom tells you to take out the garbage and you grab it, slam the door, stomp out of the house, and leave the garbage by the curb, you obeyed her, but you didn't honor her. Honor has to do with your attitude.

You don't honor your parents because they deserve it; you don't honor them because you like or dislike their rules. You honor them because of their position. It's a lot like the way people treat the president of the United States. They honor him even if they don't like the clothes he wears or the policies he practices.

The great thing about honor is that it comes with **an incredible promise.** If you honor your mother and father, you will pave the way to a great relationship with your mom and dad, and God will bless you for it. Choose today to honor them.

Lord, forgive me for not giving my mom and dad the honor they deserve. I choose to hold them in high regard because of the position they have. In Jesus' name. Amen.

A father of the fatherless, a defender of widows,
is God in His holy habitation.

—PSALM 68:5

But as many as received Him, to them He gave
the right to become children of God, to those who
believe in His name.

—JOHN 1:12

"I will be a Father to you,
And you shall be My sons and daughters,"
Says the LORD Almighty.

—2 CORINTHIANS 6:18

And my God shall supply all your need
according to His riches in glory by Christ Jesus.

—PHILIPPIANS 4:19

HOW TO

Deal with Divorce

Many young people feel like orphans. They feel distant from one or both parents because of a divorce, or they feel abandoned because they never met their mom or dad. If either of these describes you, then remember these promises: God **promises** to be your parent (Ps. 68:5), and He **promises** to fill all your needs (Phil. 4:19). You can hold on to these promises, knowing that God never makes a promise that He won't keep.

Some young people get stuck in the middle of a bitter divorce. If this happens to you and your mom and dad are putting each other down, don't agree with them. Pray for them. Realize that your parents aren't perfect. Try to see them *not* as your parents, but as human beings who need the touch of God's grace on their lives.

Lord, I thank you that even in the midst of my despair, even in the midst of my broken family, you care about me. Lord, I reach out to you to be my parent. I ask you to bring people into my life who can give me the kind of leadership and guidance that I need. In Jesus' name. Amen.

While Jesus was still talking to the multi-tudes, behold, His mother and brothers stood out-side, seeking to speak with Him. Then one said to Him, "Look, Your mother and Your brothers are standing outside, seeking to speak with You." But He answered and said to the one who told Him, "Who is My mother and who are My brothers?" And He stretched out His hand toward His disciples and said, "Here are My mother and My brothers! For whoever does the will of My Father in heaven is My brother and sister and mother."

—MATTHEW 12:46–50

For as we have many members in one body, but all the members do not have the same function, so we, being many, are one body in Christ, and indi-vidually members of one another.

—ROMANS 12:4–5

Love suffers long and is kind; love does not envy; love does not parade itself, is not puffed up; does not behave rudely, does not seek its own, is not provoked, thinks no evil; does not rejoice in iniquity, but rejoices in the truth; bears all things, believes all things, hopes all things, endures all things. Love never fails.

—1 CORINTHIANS 13:4–8

HOW TO
Get Along with
Stepparents

Many young people feel that a stepparent isn't a "real" parent, and their defensive attitude keeps the stepparent out of their lives. Sure, it's not easy when someone new comes into your family but consider this: Jesus also had a stepfather. Jesus knew who His real Father was, yet he accepted Joseph's input into His life.

Jesus' definition of family is much different from ours. While on earth, Jesus looked at the people around Him and said that His family was made up of anyone who followed **God's will.**

You may have a stepparent in your home right now. They might not be your blood relative, but if they love God and are doing their best to nurture you, then they really are a true part of your family, as Jesus defines it. If you can open up to your stepparent, you may be amazed at the miracle that will occur in your family.

Lord, I choose to honor the adults in my life. Forgive me for any hurtful words that I've said to my stepparent. Lord, make us into a true family whose hearts are all living for you. In Jesus' name. Amen.

Extreme
Promises

Of

Guidance

Yea, though I walk through the valley of the
    shadow of death,
I will fear no evil;
For You are with me;
Your rod and Your staff, they comfort me.

—PSALM 23:4

For He shall give His angels charge over you,
To keep you in all your ways.

—PSALM 91:11

For God has not given us a spirit of fear, but of
power and of love and of a sound mind.

—2 TIMOTHY 1:7

So we may boldly say:
"The LORD is my helper;
I will not fear.
What can man do to me?"

—HEBREWS 13:6

There is no fear in love; but perfect love casts
out fear, because fear involves torment. But he
who fears has not been made perfect in love.

—1 JOHN 4:18

WHAT TO DO
When You Fear

Fear is not just a feeling; it is a **spirit** (2 Tim. 1:7). It is not just a thought; it is a spiritual force. If you are feeling afraid, then you must rebuke the spirit of fear. Because you are a Christian, Jesus has given you the authority over all manner of evil.

Take a look into God's Word, and begin to memorize verses that talk about not being afraid. When you realize that He is with you, that He'd never leave you or forsake you, what do you have to be afraid of? The point is to focus on the *promise* not on the *fear*. Quit trying *not* to be afraid, and focus on the Truth.

Lord, I thank you that I do not have to live in fear. I rebuke the spirit of fear in your name. You are with me in the midst of every storm; as a result, I will not be afraid. In Jesus' name. Amen.

When you pass through the waters, I will be
    with you;
And through the rivers, they shall not overflow
    you.
When you walk through the fire, you shall not
    be burned,
Nor shall the flame scorch you.

—ISAIAH 43:2

He is a double-minded man, unstable in all
his ways.

—JAMES 1:8

For where envy and self-seeking exist, confusion and every evil thing are there. But the
wisdom that is from above is first pure, then
peaceable, gentle, willing to yield, full of mercy
and good fruits, without partiality and without
hypocrisy. Now the fruit of righteousness is sown
in peace by those who make peace.

—JAMES 3:16–18

WHAT TO DO
When You Doubt

Some young people only go to church because their parents make them. Some only believe in God and Jesus because their parents do or because the pastor says that it's a good thing to do. But in everyday life, they **live in doubt** because they are relying on someone else's faith and not on their own.

If you have doubts about your salvation, or about God's goodness, then ask yourself: *Do I have a connection with Jesus that is my own?* When you really know Him, a confidence floods your heart that can't be described with human words. Have you completely opened yourself up and committed the deepest part of yourself to Him?

If you want to turn your doubt into faith, then **get to know God** through His Word—read it, meditate on it, and say it to yourself again and again. As you do this, your faith will grow, and your doubt will fade away.

Lord, I thank you that you are my Savior. I put my life in your hands, and I choose to build my faith by knowing your Word. In Jesus' name. Amen.

Wait on the LORD;
Be of good courage,
And He shall strengthen your heart;
Wait, I say, on the LORD!

—PSALM 27:14

The end of a thing is better than its beginning;
The patient in spirit is better than the proud
in spirit.
Do not hasten in your spirit to be angry,
For anger rests in the bosom of fools.

—ECCLESIASTES 7:8–9

The LORD is good to those who wait for Him,
To the soul who seeks Him.
It is good that one should hope and wait quietly
For the salvation of the LORD.

—LAMENTATIONS 3:25–26

But if we hope for what we do not see, we eagerly wait for it with perseverance.

Likewise the Spirit also helps in our weaknesses. For we do not know what we should pray for as we ought, but the Spirit Himself makes intercession for us with groanings which cannot be uttered.

—ROMANS 8:25–26

WHAT TO DO
When You Are Stressed

- You are about to play in that championship ball game.
- You are studying for your college entrance exam.
- You are preparing for a job interview.

In each of these situations, you must be at your best. As a result, you may feel **stressed out** and anxious, and you may even forget all about God. You may be thinking, *I can do this on my own power.*

If you are anxious, then you are relying on yourself rather than on the Lord. It's time to let go and let Him take over. God wants to be involved in every part of your life!

Philippians 4:8 gives the **perfect remedy** to relieve stress: "Whatever things are true, . . . noble, . . . just, . . . pure, . . . lovely, . . . if there is anything praiseworthy—meditate on these things." Write this entire Scripture down, and take it with you. Choose to think on these things, and God will flood your heart with peace.

Lord, forgive me for relying on myself. I turn my anxiety and stress over to you. I thank you for flooding my mind with peace right now. In Jesus' name. Amen.

As far as the east is from the west,
So far has He removed our transgressions from us.

—PSALM 103:12

Therefore if the Son sets you free, you shall be free indeed.

—JOHN 8:36

For sin shall not have dominion over you, for you are not under law but under grace.

—ROMANS 6:14

Do not be conformed to this world, but be transformed by the renewing of your mind, that you may prove what is that good and acceptable and perfect will of God.

—ROMANS 12:2

WHAT TO DO
When You Sin

So you've **blown it.** You're mad at yourself because you've done it again. Maybe it's the same sin as the last time. You asked for forgiveness, and now you feel embarrassed to come back to God again.

Although the devil may be trying to make you feel like you are a slave to your sin, you are not. Jesus died to set you free. John 8:36 says, "Therefore if the Son sets you free, you shall be free indeed." And Romans 6:14 says that sin is *not* your master.

Remember, too, that 1 John 1:9 says, "If we confess our sins, He is faithful and just to forgive us." When you say "Lord forgive me," He forgives you each time. He **makes you clean.** When you ask for forgiveness, your sin is cast "as far as the east is from the west" (Ps. 103:12); He separates you from your sin.

Repent from your sin, and then thank God for delivering you from it. You are free!

Lord Jesus, I thank you for your promise, and I confess to you that I have blown it again. Forgive me, cleanse me, and set me free from this sin. In your name. Amen.

Therefore know that the LORD your God, He is God, the faithful God who keeps covenant and mercy for a thousand generations with those who love Him and keep His commandments.

—DEUTERONOMY 7:9

As for God, His way is perfect;
The word of the LORD is proven;
He is a shield to all who trust in Him.
For who is God, except the LORD?
And who is a rock, except our God?
It is God who arms me with strength,
And makes my way perfect.

—PSALM 18:30–32

"For the mountains shall depart
And the hills be removed,
But My kindness shall not depart from you,
Nor shall My covenant of peace be removed,"
Says the LORD, who has mercy on you.

—ISAIAH 54:10

WHAT TO DO
When You Are Uncertain
about God

Have you ever been talking with friends when suddenly you are asked what you think of a certain person? "Well," you say, "I don't know that person well enough to say." Then, in a different conversation, you hear people accusing a friend of doing something wrong. This time, you say, "Absolutely not. I know that person wouldn't do that!" You speak with confidence because you really **know** your friend.

When you feel uncertain about God, it may be an indication that you really don't know Him that well. You don't understand His character or His nature. Or maybe you **know** *about* Him. Maybe you prayed to give your heart to Him, but you haven't gotten to know him like a friend.

When you read Psalm 18:30–32, you can tell that David really knew God. He knew God's heart. I encourage you to memorize this Scripture today. This is the God you serve! Go on an adventure to really get to know Him, not just know *about* Him.

Lord, forgive me for not knowing you very well. I want to be your friend. I will dive into your Word so that I can get to know you. In Jesus' name. Amen.

Bless the Lord, O my soul,
And forget not all His benefits:
Who forgives all your iniquities,
Who heals all your diseases,
Who redeems your life from destruction,
Who crowns you with lovingkindness and
tender mercies.

—PSALM 103:2–4

I, even I, am He who blots out your transgressions for My own sake;
And I will not remember your sins.

—ISAIAH 43:25

Brethren, I do not count myself to have appre-
hended; but one thing I do, forgetting those
things which are behind and reaching forward to
those things which are ahead, I press toward the
goal for the prize of the upward call of God in
Christ Jesus.

—PHILIPPIANS 3:13–14

WHAT TO DO
When You Have
Regrets

Regrets are hard to let go of. We beat ourselves up over them. Often, these are things that we have done to other people. We bring up these **past sins** to God again and again, asking for forgiveness over and over. We seem to forget that God says, "I will not remember your sins" (Isa. 43:25). When we ask Him for forgiveness for something a second time, he says, "What are you talking about? I don't even remember your sin because I already forgave you."

Sometimes, we know that God has forgiven us but we haven't forgiven ourselves. But the only way to deal with regret is to **let go** of your past, to forgive yourself. Think about it: If God—the Creator of the universe—has forgiven you and cleansed you, then surely you can forgive yourself. Let God's love and grace fill you as you except His forgiveness by forgiving yourself.

Lord Jesus, I'm so tired of dealing with this regret. Thank you for forgiving me. I choose to forgive myself and let go of the past. In your name. Amen.

A man's heart plans his way,
But the Lord directs his steps.

—Proverbs 16:9

Then the word of the Lord came to me, saying:
"Before I formed you in the womb I knew you;
Before you were born I sanctified you;
I ordained you a prophet to the nations."

—Jeremiah 1:4–5

To him the doorkeeper opens, and the sheep hear his voice; and he calls his own sheep by name and leads them out. And when he brings out his own sheep, he goes before them; and the sheep follow him, for they know his voice.

—John 10:3–4

If any of you lacks wisdom, let him ask of God, who gives to all liberally and without reproach, and it will be given to him. But let him ask in faith, with no doubting, for he who doubts is like a wave of the sea driven and tossed by the wind.

—James 1:5–6

WHAT TO DO
About God's Will For Your Life

God has an incredible plan for your life! In the Bible, the Lord says, "Before you were even in your mother's womb, I orchestrated an amazing life for you!" (paraphrase of Jer. 1:4–5). But how do you find out what that plan is? First, you need to learn how to **recognize His voice,** and you can do that by reading His Word. As you read His Word, you will begin to understand the kinds of things that God says.

Then, when you hear Him, you'll say, "Oh, there it is. It's the same voice I hear in the Bible. It's God." It may not come as a loud bang. It may not sound like thunder from heaven. But the voice of the living God will move your heart, and you will know it is Him because you have been listening to Him in your quiet time when you read your Bible.

Lord, I thank you that I am your sheep and that I can recognize your voice. I commit to reading and studying your Word so that I will know your will for my life. In Jesus' name. Amen.

Trust in the LORD with all your heart,
And lean not on your own understanding;
In all your ways acknowledge Him,
And He shall direct your paths.

—PROVERBS 3:5–6

The simple believes every word,
But the prudent considers well his steps.

—PROVERBS 14:15

For everyone who asks receives, and he who seeks finds, and to him who knocks, it will be opened.

—LUKE 11:10

But God has revealed them to us through His Spirit. For the Spirit searches all things, yes, the deep things of God.

—1 CORINTHIANS 2:10

Be diligent to present yourself approved to God, a worker who does not need to be ashamed, rightly dividing the word of truth.

—2 TIMOTHY 2:15

WHAT TO DO About Right Choices

Life is full of choices. As a teenager, you are faced with choices everyday, such as who your friends are, what you're going to do with your life, what sports you will play.

Many young people who are trying to make a decision pray, "Lord, what should I do?" Then after about ten seconds, they make their decision. They don't wait because they don't know what they are waiting for. What should they expect? Maybe something written in the sky or an audible voice? The fact is, the answer is already available in God's Word. If you take **biblical principles** and apply them to the decisions you need to make, then you invite God's blessing on your life.

Instead of going on a hunch or a gut feeling, we need to give thought to our steps. We need to consider God's plan. Remember that God's will never goes against His own principles, which are spelled out in His Word. With any choice you make, you should be able to back up your decision with a Scripture verse.

Lord, I thank you for giving me wisdom in your Word. I commit to diving into your Word before I make any decision. In Jesus' name. Amen.

Extreme Promises about

Jesus

For God so loved the world that He gave His only begotten Son, that whoever believes in Him should not perish but have everlasting life.

—John 3:16

Even the righteousness of God, through faith in Jesus Christ, to all and on all who believe. For there is no difference; for all have sinned and fall short of the glory of God, being justified freely by His grace through the redemption that is in Christ Jesus.

—Romans 3:22–24

For by grace you have been saved through faith, and that not of yourselves; it is the gift of God, not of works, lest anyone should boast.

—Ephesians 2:8–9

Not by works of righteousness which we have done, but according to His mercy He saved us, through the washing of regeneration and renewing of the Holy Spirit, whom He poured out on us abundantly through Jesus Christ our Savior.

—Titus 3:5–6

HE IS

Your Savior

It's easy for us to say, "Jesus is my Savior." The question is, Savior of what? Think about it for a moment. What has He *really* saved us from? Sometimes the word *savior* is used so often that we have forgotten what it means.

Yes, He has saved us from sin and destruction, and He has saved us from hell. But we forget that He is also saving us from the "garbage" of this life, here and now. **He saves us** from living with pain. He puts us back together when we fall apart. **He saves us** from a relationship that is destructive. **He saves us** from hopelessness, despair, and loneliness. **He saves us** from our past—from all the things that we have done to mess ourselves up.

What an incredible God! He gave His life on the cross, shedding His blood to save us from all the things that we have done, are doing, and will do to mess up our lives.

Take this moment to celebrate that Jesus really is your **Savior**.

Lord Jesus, thank you for really being my Savior and for rescuing me from the things of this world. In your name. Amen.

I beseech you therefore, brethren, by the mercies of God, that you present your bodies a living sacrifice, holy, acceptable to God, which is your reasonable service. And do not be conformed to this world, but be transformed by the renewing of your mind, that you may prove what is that good and acceptable and perfect will of God.

—ROMANS 12:1–2

Or do you not know that your body is the temple of the Holy Spirit who is in you, whom you have from God, and you are not your own? For you were bought at a price; therefore glorify God in your body and in your spirit, which are God's.

—1 CORINTHIANS 6:19–20

God has highly exalted Him and given Him the name which is above every name, that at the name of Jesus every knee should bow, of those in heaven, and of those on earth, and of those under the earth, and that every tongue should confess that Jesus Christ is Lord, to the glory of God the Father.

—PHILIPPIANS 2:9–11

HE IS
Your Lord

The word *lord* means boss, leader, or commander in chief.

It is easy for us to say that Jesus is our Lord, but let's think about that statement. We say it, but we still let other people or other things govern lives. For some people, movies or high-tech games are the focus of their lives. For several others, peer pressure determines their behavior, and they let friends tell them what to do. And for still others, money rules over them. As a result, these things become their "lord."

When other people or other things become our master rather than Jesus, we are missing out on the life He intends for us—He wants to give us **abundant life!** Now is the time to think about the chief influence in your life. Is it Jesus? Or is it other people and other things? He wants to be first in your life.

Lord Jesus, forgive me for letting other things influence and dominate me and control my life. Today, I make you my Lord, the leader of my life. Amen.

But God demonstrates His own love toward us, in that while we were still sinners, Christ died for us.

—ROMANS 5:8

And now abide faith, hope, love, these three; but the greatest of these is love.

—1 CORINTHIANS 13:13

That Christ may dwell in your hearts through faith; that you, being rooted and grounded in love, may be able to comprehend with all the saints what is the width and length and depth and height—to know the love of Christ which passes knowledge; that you may be filled with all the fullness of God.

—EPHESIANS 3:17–19

HE IS
Your Love

We live in a love-starved world. Parents and young people have such busy schedules that they don't have time to really love one other, and many young people have so many shallow friendships that they don't know how to have deeper relationships.

But only Jesus can love you perfectly and fully. He wants to love you like you have always wanted to be loved. The Bible says that **God is love** (1 John 4:8)—He is made out of the stuff. If you stay close to God, then you will be close to His love. In fact, you can't be near Jesus without getting love all over you. It's His nature. It's who He is. In fact, He *made* you to *love* you.

Not many people really know what it feels like to be loved by supernatural love. You don't have to look to anybody else to find it. He is waiting to fill your heart with the incredible warmth of accepting, heavenly love.

Lord Jesus, I thank you for loving me no matter what I do or say. In the midst of this busy world, I look to you to be the lover of my soul. In your name. Amen.

A man who has friends must himself be
    friendly,
But there is a friend who sticks closer than a
    brother.

—PROVERBS 18:24

This is My commandment, that you love one
another as I have loved you. Greater love has no one
than this, than to lay down one's life for his friends.
You are My friends if you do whatever I command
you. No longer do I call you servants, for a servant
does not know what his master is doing; but I have
called you friends, for all things that I heard from
My Father I have made known to you. You did not
choose Me, but I chose you and appointed you that
you should go and bear fruit, and that your fruit
should remain, that whatever you ask the Father in
My name He may give you.

—JOHN 15:12–16

But if we walk in the light as He is in the
light, we have fellowship with one another, and
the blood of Jesus Christ His Son cleanses us from
all sin.

—1 JOHN 1:7

Behold, I stand at the door and knock. If anyone hears My voice and opens the door, I will come
in to him and dine with him, and he with Me.

—REVELATION 3:20

HE IS
Your Friend

Most of the time, we hear that Jesus wants to be our Lord and Savior. But did you know that He also wants to be your **Friend?**

It may seem amazing that the Son of God, who gave His life for us and who dominates the universe, would also want to be our friend, but Jesus says, "I have called you friends" (John 15:15).

We've all had friends we thought we could count on but who let us down. Jesus is different. He is a friend who "sticks closer than a brother" (Prov. 18:24). He will never give up on you and will never let you down. Yes, He wants to be your Lord, but He also wants to be your intimate Friend. So, how does that work? When you pray, you can share your heart and secret thoughts with Him; then quiet yourself and listen to His caring response. Nurture His friendship each day.

Lord, I thank you that you want to be my friend and that you care about the deepest part of me. When it seems that no one else has the time, I know that you want to listen. In Jesus' name. Amen.

And be found in Him, not having my own righteousness, which is from the law, but that which is through faith in Christ, the righteousness which is from God by faith; that I may know Him and the power of His resurrection, and the fellowship of His sufferings, being conformed to His death, if, by any means, I may attain to the resurrection from the dead.

—PHILIPPIANS 3:9–11

That by two immutable things, in which it is impossible for God to lie, we might have strong consolation, who have fled for refuge to lay hold of the hope set before us. This hope we have as an anchor of the soul, both sure and steadfast, and which enters the Presence behind the veil.

—HEBREWS 6:18–19

Blessed be the God and Father of our Lord Jesus Christ, who according to His abundant mercy has begotten us again to a living hope through the resurrection of Jesus Christ from the dead.

—1 PETER 1:3

HE IS
Your Hope

Where is your hope?

Too many people put their hope in a friend or boyfriend or girlfriend. They think that person will always love them and will never let them down, but then they are **disappointed** when the relationship ends.

Other people put their hope in things. They say, "If I can just get that car . . . or that new stereo . . . or that new outfit, then my life will be great." But when they get it, they still feel empty.

Some young people put their hope in their parents. They believe that their parents will always be there for them, but when they find out that their parents aren't perfect, it hurts.

Jesus wants to be our hope. He wants to be the one we look to for absolute **fulfillment,** the one we can depend on. If we put our hope in other people or other things, we will always be disappointed, but if we put our hope in Jesus, He will never let us down.

Lord Jesus, I thank you that I can depend on you. You will never shatter my hope. I know that when I pursue you, you will fill me up. In your name. Amen.

Yet it shall not be so among you; but whoever desires to become great among you shall be your servant. And whoever of you desires to be first shall be slave of all. For even the Son of Man did not come to be served, but to serve, and to give His life a ransom for many.

—MARK 10:43–45

Let this mind be in you which was also in Christ Jesus, who, being in the form of God, did not consider it robbery to be equal with God, but made Himself of no reputation, taking the form of a bondservant, and coming in the likeness of men. And being found in appearance as a man, He humbled Himself and became obedient to the point of death, even the death of the cross.

—PHILIPPIANS 2:5–8

Looking unto Jesus, the author and finisher of our faith, who for the joy that was set before Him endured the cross, despising the shame, and has sat down at the right hand of the throne of God.

—HEBREWS 12:2

For to this you were called, because Christ also suffered for us, leaving us an example, that you should follow His steps.

—1 PETER 2:21

HE IS Your Example

Think of all of the **examples** in our society today: rock 'n' roll heroes, athletes, movie stars, wrestling heroes, even cartoon characters. These examples may not be noble or honorable, but if they are cool and popular, then the world likes them. Unfortunately, if we imitate their behavior and lifestyle, then our lives become just as chaotic and confused as theirs.

If we let Him, Jesus Christ can be a perfect model for our lives. If you put your trust in Him and look to Him as your example, then nothing that anyone else says or does can cause you to be led astray.

"WWJD?" is a popular slogan today. It stands for "What would Jesus do?" In any situation, we can look to Him for an example. We should ask, How would He love? How would He care? How would His heart reach out?

Lord Jesus, I thank you that you've given me a perfect example of how to live. I commit to looking to you as the chief example for my life. In your name. Amen.

My sheep hear My voice, and I know them, and they follow Me. And I give them eternal life, and they shall never perish; neither shall anyone snatch them out of My hand. My Father, who has given them to Me, is greater than all; and no one is able to snatch them out of My Father's hand. I and My Father are one.

—John 10:27–30

Who also has sealed us and given us the Spirit in our hearts as a guarantee.

—2 Corinthians 1:22

And do not grieve the Holy Spirit of God, by whom you were sealed for the day of redemption.

—Ephesians 4:30

Now to Him who is able to keep you from
    stumbling,
And to present you faultless
Before the presence of His glory with exceed-
    ing joy,
To God our Savior,
Who alone is wise,
Be glory and majesty,
Dominion and power,
Both now and forever.

—Jude 24–25

HE IS

Your Security

What can you really count on these days? In a popular television commercial, Chevrolet says its trucks are "like a rock." Why do they use this slogan? Because they want us to think that their trucks are as solid and steadfast as rocks—a solid rock never wears out or changes.

The Bible says that Jesus is our rock (Ps. 18:2). When everything in this world changes—people, circumstances, government—Jesus stays the same. Sometimes people's personalities change, even when you never thought they would. But His nature and His character never vary. When things seem to be passing by you in a **whirlwind,** you can stand on the **Rock** and never be shaken.

Lord Jesus, in this world built on shifting sand, I thank you that I can build my life on you—the Rock, because you will never change. In your name. Amen.

The Spirit of the Lord God is upon Me,
Because the Lord has anointed Me
To preach good tidings to the poor;
He has sent Me to heal the brokenhearted,
To proclaim liberty to the captives,
And the opening of the prison to those who
    are bound.

—ISAIAH 61:1

Therefore if the Son makes you free, you shall
be free indeed.

—JOHN 8:36

For the law of the Spirit of life in Christ Jesus
has made me free from the law of sin and death.

—ROMANS 8:2

Now the Lord is the Spirit; and where the Spirit
of the Lord is, there is liberty.

—2 CORINTHIANS 3:17

HE IS
Your Deliverer

Jesus says that He came to set us free, but when Jesus looks at humanity, He sees people who are slaves. Too many people are in a jail of sin, but they think that they are free to do whatever they want. In reality, the more they express their freedom, the more enslaved they become.

The sad part is that most people don't even know they are slaves. Many people who have given their lives to the Lord have this "poor me" mentality and think they will never really live free of sin. They sit inside their **jail cell** and act like they can't get out. Imagine how that must make Jesus feel. **He died** to set us free, yet we stay in prison and act like we are still slaves.

He has set you free. Through Jesus, you have been given the key to open the jail door. He has delivered you from sin and from every habit and every kind of corruption. Go and live like a free person.

Lord Jesus, I thank you that in giving your life, you paid the price to set me free. I refuse to live like a slave anymore. In your name. Amen.

The LORD will give strength to His people;
The LORD will bless His people with peace.

—PSALM 29:11

You will keep him in perfect peace,
Whose mind is stayed on You,
Because he trusts in You.

—ISAIAH 26:3

Therefore, having been justified by faith, we
have peace with God through our Lord Jesus Christ.

—ROMANS 5:1

And let the peace of God rule in your hearts,
to which also you were called in one body; and be
thankful.

—COLOSSIANS 3:15

HE IS
Your Peace

One of the names of Jesus is "Prince of Peace" (Is. 9:6). You can't have peace without having Jesus in your life. You can try drugs or alcohol, but you won't feel peace. You can listen to music or fill your life with many activities, but you won't find peace.

Every human soul is **looking for peace.** To find it, you gotta go to the one who invented it: the Prince of Peace.

Your life may seem busy or fun, but if you still feel a longing in your heart when you are all alone in your bed, then look at some of the Scriptures on the opposite page and say them aloud. Ask Jesus to make them true in your life, and then let the powerful peace of God's presence settle on you.

Lord, even though the world is full of confusion, I can be full of peace because you are my Lord. You're the center of my life, and I will take your Word and put it into my heart and receive your peace. In Jesus' name. Amen.

Blessed be the God and Father of our Lord Jesus Christ, who has blessed us with every spiritual blessing in the heavenly places in Christ.

—EPHESIANS 1:3

Now to Him who is able to do exceedingly abundantly above all that we ask or think, according to the power that works in us, to Him be glory in the church by Christ Jesus to all generations, forever and ever. Amen.

—EPHESIANS 3:20–21

I can do all things through Christ who strengthens me.

—PHILIPPIANS 4:13

And whatever we ask we receive from Him, because we keep His commandments and do those things that are pleasing in His sight. And this is His commandment: that we should believe on the name of His Son Jesus Christ and love one another, as He gave us commandment.

—1 JOHN 3:22–23

HE IS

Your Everything

The Bible says the Lord is our "all in all" (Eph. 1:23). A lot of people accept Jesus as their Savior, but their lives still revolve around other things. They get their zest in life from their job, or a sport that they play, or the band that they are into. Jesus is really just another attachment to their life. He is sort of another club that they go to, like Wednesday night youth group.

There is no fulfillment like what you get when you **focus on Jesus.** When He is the center of your life, everything else pales in comparison. Extracurricular activities don't matter as much, sports aren't as important, and your work takes a backseat. When you've got Him, you've really got it "all." Our joy comes from knowing that He is the purpose of our life.

Lord, I thank you for being my all in all. Forgive me, Lord, for trying to find fulfillment in other things. From now on, you are the center of my life, the driving passion in my heart. In Jesus' name. Amen.

Extreme Promises

Of

For thus says the Lord of hosts: "He sent Me after glory, to the nations which plunder you; for he who touches you touches the apple of His eye."

—ZECHARIAH 2:8

Likewise the Spirit also helps in our weaknesses. For we do not know what we should pray for as we ought, but the Spirit Himself makes intercession for us with groaning which cannot be uttered. Now He who searches the hearts knows what the mind of the Spirit is, because He makes intercession for the saints according to the will of God.

—ROMANS 8:26–27

In whom we have boldness and access with confidence through faith in Him.

—EPHESIANS 3:12

WHAT TO DO
When You Don't Feel Important

In the beginning, after God made the animals and the earth, He still wanted to create one more special being. He wanted to create someone that He could love, someone who could appreciate His love and who could love Him back. So He created Adam and then Eve, human beings made in His image.

You were born to be loved by God. You were born with a **bull's-eye** painted on you, and God is aiming His love right at it. It doesn't really matter if you are important to anyone else because you are important to God. Like Zechariah, you can know that you are "apple of His eye" (2:8).

There is nothing you can do to make Him love you any less or any more. He loves you with all the love in the universe.

Lord, I thank you that no matter what people say or do to me or how they make me feel, I am important to you. Thank you, Lord, that I am the object of your affection today. In Jesus' name. Amen.

The righteous cry out, and the LORD hears,
And delivers them out of all their troubles.

—PSALM 34:17

I will lift up my eyes to the hills—
From whence comes my help?
My help comes from the LORD,
Who made heaven and earth.

—PSALM 121:1-2

Though I walk in the midst of trouble, You will
        revive me;
You will stretch out Your hand
Against the wrath of my enemies,
And Your right hand will save me.

—PSALM 138:7

The LORD is good,
A stronghold in the day of trouble;
And He knows those who trust in Him.

—NAHUM 1:7

WHAT TO DO
When Troubles Hit
Your Life

Some people think that when they become a Christian, their troubles will end. But the Bible doesn't promise an easy road. Instead, it promises something even better: **God's love and help.** When troubles hit David, he said, "I will lift up my eyes to the hills . . . My help comes from the LORD" (Ps. 121:1–2). In other words, David quit looking *down* at the problem and began looking *up* for help.

When troubles hit your life, do you respond in fear or in faith? If you turn your eyes upward, you can focus on God and His ability to help you. But if you dwell on the trouble in fear, then you will begin a downward spiral toward depression.

Today, no matter what happens, lift up your eyes "to the hills." Remember He's the mighty creator God, and if He can *create hills*, then he certainly can help you with whatever troubles come your way.

Lord, I praise you for being my Creator and for being so good. I don't have to live in fear. I choose to live in faith, believing that you are on my side and you will rescue me. In Jesus' name. Amen.

But He was wounded for our transgressions,
He was bruised for our iniquities;
The chastisement for our peace was upon
    Him,
And by His stripes we are healed.

—ISAIAH 53:5

Heal me, O Lord, and I shall be healed;
Save me, and I shall be saved,
For You are my praise.

—JEREMIAH 17:14

And whatever things you ask in prayer, believing, you will receive.

—MATTHEW 2:22

Is anyone among you sick? Let him call for the elders of the church, and let them pray over him, anointing him with oil in the name of the Lord. And the prayer of faith will save the sick, and the Lord will raise him up. And if he has committed sins, he will be forgiven.

—JAMES 5:14–15

WHAT TO DO
When You Are
Physically
Sick

When you're sick, pray for healing. But don't pray and then wonder if it will happen. Pray with confidence. **Pray with faith,** believing that God is able and willing to heal you.

Jesus always prayed with confidence, knowing that His Father was listening. The Bible also says people who are sick should ask the elders of the church for their "prayer of faith" (James 15:15). In 3 John 2, the apostle John says, "I pray that you may prosper in all things and be in health, just as your soul prospers." John knew that God wants our souls as well as our bodies to prosper.

God is looking for faith to be the strength of your prayer. Acknowledge with confidence that He is a healing God and ask for His healing touch.

Lord Jesus, I thank you that you are the God who heals. You said a prayer of faith will raise up the sick. I believe that you can give me a supernatural miracle right now and can heal me. In your name. Amen.

Be strong and of good courage, do not fear nor be afraid of them; for the Lord your God, He is the One who goes with you. He will not leave you nor forsake you.

—Deuteronomy 31:6

How precious is Your lovingkindness, O God! Therefore the children of men put their trust under the shadow of Your wings.

—Psalm 36:7

Because he has set his love upon Me, therefore
    I will deliver him;
I will set him on high, because he has known
    My name.
He shall call upon Me, and I will answer him;
I will be with him in trouble;
I will deliver him and honor him.

—Psalm 91:14–15

Teaching them to observe all things that I have commanded you; and lo, I am with you always, even to the end of the age.

—Matthew 28:20

WHAT TO DO
When You Feel Deserted

Many times we feel deserted when someone lets us down. But Jesus said, "I will never leave you nor forsake you" (Heb. 13:5). In many places throughout the Bible, we are told that God is always with us.

If we put our expectation in a person, that person will disappoint us sooner or later. We need to **shift our expectancy** and put our confidence in His Word, not in the word of another person.

Lord, I put my expectation in you today. I thank you that you'll never desert me. Even though I can't see you with my physical eyes, I can sense you with the eyes of my heart. In Jesus' name. Amen.

As for God, His way is perfect;
The word of the LORD is proven;
He is a shield to all who trust in Him.

—PSALM 18:30

"For My thoughts are not your thoughts,
Nor are your ways My ways," says the LORD.
"For as the heavens are higher than the earth,
So are My ways higher than your ways,
And My thoughts than your thoughts."

—ISAIAH 55:8–9

And I will make an everlasting covenant with them, that I will not turn away from doing them good; but I will put My fear in their hearts so that they will not depart from Me.

—JEREMIAH 32:40

Let us hold fast the confession of our hope without wavering, for He who promised is faithful.

—HEBREWS 10:23

extreme promises of help

WHAT TO DO
When You Don't Understand
God's Ways

Some people lose their faith when things don't go like they think they should. They are quick to say that God let them down or that other Christians let them down, but they don't see the **big picture** of all that God is doing. Other people think they know all that there is to know about God, but when things don't line up with what they know, they think something must be wrong with God.

It is in these times that we must trust in the character and nature of our God. You can see it woven all throughout the Scripture: He is a good God, He protects His children, He takes good care of us, and He gave His own Son so that we could be rescued. Even if you don't understand the circumstances in your life right now, put your confidence in the character of God.

Lord, I thank you that even though I don't understand my circumstances, I know your nature. You're a good God, and you're taking care of me. I know that you'll work all this together for my good because I love you with all my heart. In Jesus' name. Amen.

(97)

Our soul waits for the LORD;
He is our help and our shield.

—PSALM 33:20

I wait for the LORD, my soul waits,
And in His word I do hope.

—PSALM 130:5

For you were once darkness, but now you are
light in the Lord. Walk as children of light (for
the fruit of the Spirit is in all goodness, righteousness, and truth), finding out what is
acceptable to the Lord. And have no fellowship
with the unfruitful works of darkness, but rather
expose them.

—EPHESIANS 5:8-11

WHAT TO DO
When Nothing
Goes Right

It's been one of those days. Everything that could go wrong has gone wrong. When this happens, it's easy to feel like everyone is against you, even God. And if you're only looking at this *one* day and not at the whole picture, then sure, it can look pretty bad. But back up for a minute, and look at your life. Can you really say that nothing has gone right?

God has provided for your needs, hasn't He? Also think of all the things He has protected you from, tragedies that could have come your way. Consider all of the starving people of the world or people who live in war-torn countries. How does your life compare with theirs?

Stop for a moment and recognize all the things that **have gone right.** The fact is that God is looking out for you, and He will take care of you.

Lord, I thank you for all the things you have done to make my life go right and for all the things you have protected me from. I put my confidence in you and not in my circumstances. In Jesus' name. Amen.

We are hard pressed on every side, yet not crushed; we are perplexed, but not in despair; persecuted, but not forsaken; struck down, but not destroyed.

—2 Corinthians 4:8–9

Let us hold fast the confession of our hope without wavering, for He who promised is faithful.

—Hebrews 10:23

Beloved, do not think it strange concerning the fiery trial which is to try you, as though some strange thing happened to you.

—1 Peter 4:12

And now, little children, abide in Him, that when He appears, we may have confidence and not be ashamed before Him at His coming.

—1 John 2:28

WHAT TO DO
When Life is Hard

Challenges in life are the enemy's way of trying to discourage our faith. Satan tries to make us think that we are weak and feeble. Then when we hit a **rough spot,** he hopes that we'll turn into a bunch of whiners instead of turning to God.

The Scriptures say that we ought to rejoice when something goes wrong because it means that we are doing something right. It means that the devil is intimidated by what we're doing and how we're living.

When Paul was faced with trials, he said, "You know what, it seems that everything is against us, but we're not failures. We have faith, we have courage, and we're not going to back off. We're going to keep on believing" (paraphrase of 2 Cor. 4:8–9). Today, I encourage you to do the same.

Lord, I thank you that you have given me the strength to handle every kind of struggle. I thank you for the trials I am facing. I refuse to give up. In Jesus' name. Amen.

Weeping may endure for a night,
But joy comes in the morning.

—Psalm 30:5

"For I know the thoughts that I think toward you," says the Lord, "thoughts of peace and not of evil, to give you a future and a hope."

—Jeremiah 29:11

The thief does not come except to steal, and to kill, and to destroy. I have come that they may have life, and that they may have it more abundantly.

—John 10:10

We also glory in tribulations, knowing that tribulation produces perseverance; and perseverance, character; and character, hope. Now hope does not disappoint, because the love of God has been poured out in our hearts by the Holy Spirit who was given to us.

—Romans 5:5

WHAT TO DO
When Life Is Not
Worth Living

Today's teens face so many hurtful things. Some young people have been hurting for so long that they have forgotten what it feels like *not* to hurt. If that's you, you need to understand that no matter what hurt has come your way, God didn't cause it. The enemy, the devil, is the one who kills, steals, and destroys (John 10:10).

Some people think that the only way to stop hurting is to end their life. Nothing could be further from the truth. The way to stop hurting is to let God put **your broken heart back together.** That's what He said He came to do, and today, if you let him, He'll begin to do it for you. He knows your pain; let Him fix it. And talk to a parent or pastor about how you're feeling. Ask them to pray for you.

Lord Jesus, I thank you that you love me. I rebuke this spirit of death and suicide, and I ask you to give me your abundant life. I thank you for breathing your hope and your life into my heart right now. In your name. Amen.

Extreme Promises about

Your Lifestyle

You shall walk after the Lord your God and fear Him, and keep His commandments and obey His voice, and you shall serve Him and hold fast to Him.

—DEUTERONOMY 13:4

But take careful heed to do the commandment and the law which Moses the servant of the Lord commanded you, to love the Lord your God, to walk in all His ways, to keep His commandments, to hold fast to Him, and to serve Him with all your heart and with all your soul.

—JOSHUA 22:5

Be kindly affectionate to one another with brotherly love, in honor giving preference to one another; not lagging in diligence, fervent in spirit, serving the Lord. . . . distributing to the needs of the saints, given to hospitality.

—ROMANS 12:10–11, 13

For you were bought at a price; therefore glorify God in your body and in your spirit, which are God's.

—1 CORINTHIANS 6:20

Serving God

Too many Christians act more like Jesus is *their* servant instead of vice versa. They call on Him whenever they need Him, especially when they're desperate. They ask for miracles or things that they want, but they really have no intention of pursuing Him with all their heart.

The Bible tells us that we belong to Him; He purchased us with His blood (1 Cor. 6:20). If we know that we belong to Him, then we should start **acting like** we belong to Him. Our life and our future are in His hands. Instead of talking to Him at our convenience, we should exist for *His* convenience. In other words, when we realize how much He's done for us, we need to respond by serving Him in whatever way we can. Not out of obligation, or because we are trying to earn something, but out of gratitude because we are so thankful for what He has done for us.

Lord Jesus, I thank you for giving your very life for me. In return, I will serve you by giving my life to you, not out of obligation but out of gratefulness for what you have done for me. In your name. Amen.

If you diligently obey the voice of the Lord your God, to observe carefully all His commandments which I command you today, that the Lord your God will set you high above all nations of the earth. And all these blessings shall come upon you and overtake you, because you obey the voice of the Lord your God.

—DEUTERONOMY 28:1–2

I am the LORD your God,
Who teaches you to profit,
Who leads you by the way you should go.
Oh, that you had heeded My commandments!
Then your peace would have been like a river,
And your righteousness like the waves of the sea.

—ISAIAH 48:17–18

If you love Me, keep My commandments. He who has My commandments and keeps them, it is he who loves Me. And he who loves Me will be loved by My Father, and I will love him and manifest Myself to him.

—JOHN 14:15, 21

Now by this we know that we know Him, if we keep His commandments. He who says, "I know Him," and does not keep His commandments, is a liar, and the truth is not in him. But whoever keeps His word, truly the love of God is perfected in him.

—1 JOHN 2:3–5

Obedience

God is looking for young people whose hearts are so committed to Him that they want to obey Him in every way. He is looking for young people who will follow Him, even when they don't quite understand the reason for His command or instruction.

Some people think that obedience to the Lord is a chore. But the fact is, He never gives us commands to burden us; He gives us commands so that He can bless us, protect us, and take care of us. We may think that they are just rules, but really they are principles to keep us from being tricked by the devil or the world's system. Obedience is not just yelling "Jesus" out loud at a Christian concert; it's living **a life of surrender** to Him.

When you are obedient to God, you are a magnet for His blessing, and His promises will absolutely blow you away.

Lord, I thank you for promising to bless me when I obey you. Today, I commit to obeying you in all things, even when your command is hard to understand. In Jesus' name. Amen.

Let us walk properly, as in the day, not in revelry and drunkenness, not in lewdness and lust, not in strife and envy. But put on the Lord Jesus Christ, and make no provision for the flesh, to fulfill its lusts.

—ROMANS 13:13–14

Flee sexual immorality. Every sin that a man does is outside the body, but he who commits sexual immorality sins against his own body.

—1 CORINTHIANS 6:18

For this is the will of God, your sanctification: that you should abstain from sexual immorality; that each of you should know how to possess his own vessel in sanctification and honor, not in passion of lust, like the Gentiles who do not know God.

—1 THESSALONIANS 4:3–5

Marriage is honorable among all, and the bed undefiled; but fornicators and adulterers God will judge.

—HEBREWS 13:4

Unacceptable Sexual Behavior

God invented sex. From the very beginning, it was *His* idea to give a man and woman a passionate way of expressing love in a marriage. The problem is that too many people have abused sex in so many different ways that they no longer understand what it was **intended for** in the first place. Their ungodly sexual behavior has brought curses on them: it has distorted their thoughts and has hurt their bodies and hearts.

God's guidelines in the Bible are geared toward helping you have an incredible sex life when you're married. If you're a Christian, you need to keep your body pure and unpolluted from the world; only then will you enjoy the benefits of a wonderful, intimate sex life when you are married.

Lord, I commit to keeping my body and my mind free from sexual corruption. Thank you for inventing sex. Thank you for blessing my sex life in my future marriage because I am choosing to keep my mind and my body pure now. In Jesus' name. Amen.

Hear, my son, and be wise;
And guide your heart in the way.
Do not mix with winebibbers,
Or with gluttonous eaters of meat;
For the drunkard and the glutton will come to
    poverty,
And drowsiness will clothe a man with rags.

—Proverbs 23:19–21

The night is far spent, the day is at hand. Therefore let us cast off the works of darkness, and let us put on the armor of light. Let us walk properly, as in the day, not in revelry and drunkenness, not in lewdness and lust, not in strife and envy. But put on the Lord Jesus Christ, and make no provision for the flesh, to fulfill its lusts.

—Romans 13:12–14

And do not be drunk with wine, in which is dissipation; but be filled with the Spirit.

—Ephesians 5:18

Substance Abuse

When you get drunk or use drugs in any way, you are no longer in control of your brain. Once the substance gets in your system, that chemical takes over. It dominates your decisions, and you are wide open to all manner of evil—to spiritual forces of wickedness.

Some people drink or take drugs to take their minds off of their troubles, but once they are sober, those tough situations are still there. People who abuse drugs or alcohol usually feel depressed or lonely, feelings that can be traced back to when they started using the substance. That's when the spirit of loneliness or depression or some other spirit began to hover over them.

Don't take the chance. Be smart. Walk as a man or woman created in the image of God. Take control of your facilities.

Lord, I thank you that I am made in your image and that you love me. I refuse to let a chemical dominate my thinking or the way I act. In Jesus' name. Amen.

I am the true vine, and My Father is the vine-dresser. Every branch in Me that does not bear fruit He takes away; and every branch that bears fruit He prunes, that it may bear more fruit.

—JOHN 15:1–2

Therefore, as the elect of God, holy and beloved, put on tender mercies, kindness, humility, meek-ness, longsuffering; bearing with one another, and forgiving one another, if anyone has a com-plaint against another; even as Christ forgave you, so you also must do. But above all these things put on love, which is the bond of perfec-tion. And let the peace of God rule in your hearts, to which also you were called in one body; and be thankful. Let the word of Christ dwell in you richly in all wisdom, teaching and admonishing one another in psalms and hymns and spiritual songs, singing with grace in your hearts to the Lord. And whatever you do in word or deed, do all in the name of the Lord Jesus, giving thanks to God the Father through Him.

—COLOSSIANS 3:12–17

But also for this very reason, giving all dili-gence, add to your faith virtue, to virtue knowledge, to knowledge self-control, to self-control perse-verance, to perseverance godliness, to godliness brotherly kindness, and to brotherly kindness love.

—2 PETER 1:5–7

Character

When we give our lives to Jesus, we take a simple step of faith. We give Him all of our heart, and He completely changes us on the inside. **It is a miracle** that is hard to describe. Then, as we live our new life in Him, He increases our faith because He wants our lives to show the passion of our love for Him.

Unfortunately, some Christians are only skin-deep. They talk about their faith, but they still live in the same way they did before they knew Jesus. There is no evidence of change.

You don't build character overnight, but you can work on it each day. With God's help, you can deal with your weaknesses—such as lying, cheating, gossiping, or something else. As you get closer to God, people will begin to see the evidence of your faith.

God wants to develop you on the inside. Build your character by doing the things Jesus would do, even when no one else is looking.

Lord Jesus, I want more than just outward Christianity. I commit to developing my character from the deepest part of my heart. I will reflect more of you each day. In your name. Amen.

You shall not make any cuttings in your flesh for the dead, nor tattoo any marks on you: I am the LORD.

—LEVITICUS 19:28

Do you not know that you are the temple of God and that the Spirit of God dwells in you?

—1 CORINTHIANS 3:16

Do you not know that your body is the temple of the Holy Spirit who is in you, whom you have from God, and you are not your own? For you were bought at a price; therefore glorify God in your body.

—1 CORINTHIANS 6:19–20

Body Piercing and Tattoos

If you are considering getting a tattoo or piercing your body, ask yourself this very important question: *What statement am I trying to make?*

Most people with tattoos or pierced body parts are making a statement. They are saying that they don't care what anyone else thinks or that they want to be separate individuals. In reality, they are trying to identify with a music group or a clique at school, and in the process, they end up creating a wall between themselves and the outside world.

Jesus taught us to love others who are different from us, but be careful that while you're trying to reach out, you don't end up picking up ungodly attitudes. Examine your own heart and attitude.

Lord, I give you every part of my body. I commit to honor you with it. Forgive me Lord if I have picked up an attitude that has caused me to condemn Christians and push them away. Lord, I want every part of me to reflect you. In Jesus' name. Amen.

I will set nothing wicked before my eyes;
I hate the work of those who fall away;
It shall not cling to me.

—Psalm 101:3

If I have walked with falsehood,
Or if my foot has hastened to deceit,
Let me be weighed on honest scales,
That God may know my integrity.
If my step has turned from the way,
Or my heart walked after my eyes,
Or if any spot adheres to my hands,
Then let me sow, and another eat;
Yes, let my harvest be rooted out.

—Job 31:3

Finally, brethren, whatever things are true, whatever things are noble, whatever things are just, whatever things are pure, whatever things are lovely, whatever things are of good report, if there is any virtue and if there is anything praise-worthy—meditate on these things.

—Philippians 4:8

Media Influence

We constantly want something in front of our eyes to dazzle us—on the TV, on the computer, at the movies, on the Internet. It's no wonder so many people ask, "Why can't I hear God? Why isn't He speaking to me?" We have clouded our brains with so much media influence that we can't hear God speaking.

God doesn't always dazzle, but **He always fulfills.** But you've got to shut off the garbage and influence of the world long enough to hear His voice. You don't have to shut it all off or never participate in any of it, but you do need to temper it and discipline yourself. Monitor what you watch, including the Web sites you visit.

I encourage you to memorize the Scriptures on the opposite page. Paste them above your television and computer screens. The more time you spend in the Word, the easier it will be to hear God's voice.

Lord, I will spend less time with the entertainment of the world and more time with you. I will still my soul and listen for your voice. In Jesus' name. Amen.

119

Then those who feared the Lord spoke to one
   another,
And the Lord listened and heard them;
So a book of remembrance was written before
   Him
For those who fear the Lord
And who meditate on His name.

—MALACHI 3:16

Do not unequally yoked together with unbelievers. For what fellowship has righteousness
with lawlessness? And what communion has
light with darkness?

—2 CORINTHIANS 6:14

Bear one another's burdens, and so fulfill the
law of Christ. Therefore, as we have opportunity,
let us do good to all, especially to those who are
of the household of faith.

—GALATIANS 6:2, 10

Not forsaking the assembling of ourselves
together, as is the manner of some, but exhorting
one another, and so much the more as you see the
Day approaching.

—HEBREWS 10:25

Christian Fellowship

We need on-fire Christian friends around us to keep our fire going. God knows how easy it is to be influenced by people around us. That's why He tells us not to be "unequally yoked with unbelievers" (2 Cor. 6:14). Being around people who love Him *more* than you do will inspire *you* to love Him even more.

You may think that you can be a good Christian all by yourself, but many people who have tried it ended up wandering way off track, sometimes into a cult. The bottom line is: **we need Christians** around us to help us grow, to challenge us, and to push us closer to the Lord. Find a church and a youth group that you can attend on a regular basis, a place where you can get fed. Get around a bunch of other people who are passionately going after God, and you will find yourself getting stronger in Him every day.

Lord, I thank you for creating a place where I can find on-fire Christian friends and I can get fed spiritually. I want to continue to grow in faith to become the man or woman of God that you have called me to be. In Jesus' name. Amen.

And He said to them, "Go into all the world and preach the gospel to every creature."

—MARK 16:15

If a brother or sister is naked and destitute of daily food, and one of you says to them, "Depart in peace, be warmed and filled," but you do not give them the things which are needed for the body, what does it profit? Thus also faith by itself, if it does not have works, is dead.

—JAMES 2:15–17

By this we know love, because He laid down His life for us. And we also ought to lay down our lives for the brethren. But whoever has this world's goods, and sees his brother in need, and shuts up his heart from him, how does the love of God abide in him? My little children, let us not love in word or in tongue, but in deed and in truth.

—1 JOHN 3:16–18

Christian Responsibility

God wants people with heart. People who don't just say they love Jesus with their mouths, but who have a heart that really cares about the things that God cares about—people who care less about themselves and more about others.

Having a heart for **the things of God** means being responsible. Instead of just walking by people in need, you reach out to them. You realize that as a Christian, you are responsible for sharing, caring, loving, giving, and ultimately bringing people to Jesus. You don't respond simply because somebody is telling you, "Please tell this person about Jesus" or "Please give a dollar" or "Please go on a mission trip." You respond because your heart has grown big enough to sense what God wants you to do, and then you do it.

Lord, I refuse to use live a self-centered life. I choose to let my heart grow as big as yours and to reach out in compassion to those that are in need around me. In Jesus' name. Amen.

Do not lay up for yourselves treasures on earth, where moth and rust destroy and where thieves break in and steal; but lay up for yourselves treasures in heaven, where neither moth nor rust destroys and where thieves do not break in and steal. For where your treasure is, there your heart will be also.

—MATTHEW 6:19–21

Therefore be imitators of God as dear children. And walk in love, as Christ also has loved us and given Himself for us, an offering and a sacrifice to God for a sweet-smelling aroma.

—EPHESIANS 5:1–2

For I have learned in whatever state I am, to be content: I know how to be abased, and I know how to abound. Everywhere and in all things I have learned both to be full and to be hungry, both to abound and to suffer need.

—PHILIPPIANS 4:11–12

Command those who are rich in this present age not to be haughty, nor to trust in uncertain riches but in the living God, who gives us richly all things to enjoy. Let them do good, that they be rich in good works, ready to give, willing to share.

—1 TIMOTHY 6:17–18

Contentment

The world teaches us to think that the grass is greener on the other side or that we need something more to be happy. Some people work really hard to get nice things, but then when they get them, they still want **something more**. They are never content.

In Philippians, Paul basically says, "Sometimes I have a lot of stuff, and sometimes I have no stuff, but I'm content no matter what" (paraphrase of 4:11–12). His contentment had nothing to do with things. His contentment was in direct proportion to God's calling for his life. He was so involved in pursuing the vision that God had for him that sometimes he didn't even pay attention to whether he was full or hungry. He was consumed with going after God, and as a result, he was content, fulfilled, and happy, no matter what his physical circumstances were. Contentment is a **choice** you make when Jesus is the center of all that you are.

Lord, I thank you that you are my life and the center of all that I am. I refuse to listen to the world's fake promises of contentment. My fulfillment and contentment is in you. In Jesus' name. Amen.

Extreme Promises about

Prayer

Again I say to you that if two of you agree on earth concerning anything that they ask, it will be done for them by My Father in heaven.

—MATTHEW 18:19

But without faith it is impossible to please Him, for he who comes to God must believe that He is, and that He is a rewarder of those who diligently seek Him.

—HEBREWS 11:6

For let not that man suppose that he will receive anything from the Lord.

—JAMES 1:7

You ask and do not receive, because you ask amiss, that you may spend it on your pleasures.

—JAMES 4:3

HOW TO
Deal with
Unanswered
Prayer

So many Christians are frustrated because they go to God with their wish list and ask for all kinds of things but then wonder why they never get them. They don't understand why He is silent.

Sometimes we don't get what we ask for because we don't know God's will; we need to search His Word to discover it. Other times, we ask with selfish motives, forgetting that we are to put others before ourselves. Then other times, we ask for something, but we talk as though we don't really believe that God is going to answer it.

There is **a misconception** about unanswered prayer. We think the only goal of prayer is to get a bunch of stuff that we ask God for. But the goal of prayer is **to get to know Him.** He blesses us when we have sought Him with all our might.

Lord, today I am hungry for you. Fill me up with more of you as I pray. I commit to doing more than asking for my list of things; I will go after you in my prayer time to find out what you want. In Jesus' name. Amen.

The LORD has made known His salvation;
His righteousness He has revealed in the sight
of the nations.

—PSALM 98:2

Therefore pray the Lord of the harvest to send
out laborers into His harvest.

—MATTHEW 9:38

What do you think? If a man has a hundred
sheep, and one of them goes astray, does he not
leave the ninety-nine and go to the mountains
to seek the one that is straying? . . . Even so it
is not the will of your Father who is in heaven
that one of these little ones should perish.

—MATTHEW 18:12, 14

For this is good and acceptable in the sight of
God our Savior, who desires all men to be saved
and to come to the knowledge of the truth.

—1 TIMOTHY 2:3–4

HOW TO
Pray for Unsaved Loved Ones

When praying for loved ones who do not know Jesus, it is important to realize that God loves them even more than you do. It's **His heart's desire** to reach them so that they will be with Him in heaven forever. You can feel confident that He loves them because He sent His Son to die on the cross for them and for you.

Pray for your loved ones by seeing them through the eyes of God. Trust that God will move in their lives because He loves them so much and because He made them in His image—which means He designed them to spend eternity with Him!

Lord Jesus, I thank you today that you love _____ (insert the names of your loved ones who are unsaved) way more than I can ever love them. O God, send someone into their path who will reach them. Give that person the right words to open up their hearts so that they will come to know you in a very real way. I thank you that you sent your Son to die for us. I know that from the moment we are born, we are designed to be with you. In your name. Amen.

Honor your father and your mother, that your days may be long upon the land which the Lord your God is giving you.

—Exodus 20:12

Do all things without complaining and disputing, that you may become blameless and harmless, children of God without fault in the midst of a crooked and perverse generation, among whom you shine as lights in the world.

—Philippians 2:14–15

Therefore, as the elect of God, holy and beloved, put on tender mercies, kindness, humility, meekness, longsuffering; bearing with one another, and forgiving one another, if anyone has a complaint against another; even as Christ forgave you, so you also must do.

—Colossians 3:12–13

Therefore I exhort first of all that supplications, prayers, intercessions, and giving of thanks be made for all men, for kings and all who are in authority, that we may lead a quiet and peaceable life in all godliness and reverence.

—1 Timothy 2:1–2

HOW TO
Pray for Your
Family

When you are down on your knees in prayer, you are loving your family in a whole new way. You are opening the door to God's blessing about your family. Ask God to give you ideas on how to touch them and encourage them so that God's love will be **poured out** on them today.

God says to pray for those in authority over us, and of course, our mothers and fathers are our first line of authority. Ask God to bless them in their decisions, their jobs, and their marriage. Pray that God would give them supernatural wisdom as they try to be good parents and that God would minister to them.

Lord, today I pray for my mom and my dad. Give them supernatural wisdom and draw them closer to you. Please be with my whole family as they go through their activities today. Make me a blessing to them, Lord. In Jesus' name. Amen.

133

Assuredly, I say to you, whatever you bind on earth will be bound in heaven, and whatever you loose on earth will be loosed in heaven.

—MATTHEW 18:18

Behold, I give you the authority to trample on serpents and scorpions, and over all the power of the enemy, and nothing shall by any means hurt you.

—LUKE 10:19

Finally, my brethren, be strong in the Lord and in the power of His might. Put on the whole armor of God, that you may be able to stand against the wiles of the devil. For we do not wrestle against flesh and blood, but against principalities, against powers, against the rulers of the darkness of this age, against spiritual hosts of wickedness in the heavenly places. . . . Praying always with all prayer and supplication in the Spirit, being watchful to this end with all perseverance and supplication for all the saints.

—EPHESIANS 6:10–12, 18

And the Lord will deliver me from every evil work and preserve me for His heavenly kingdom. To Him be glory forever and ever. Amen!

—2 TIMOTHY 4:18

HOW TO
Prepare for Spiritual Warfare

The enemy is not playing "Mr. Nice Guy," so God is looking for Christians who are mighty and powerful in the things of the spirit.

Jesus made it very clear that we would need authority over the power of the enemy, and He gave it to us (Luke 10:19). He told us to be strong and **ready for battle** because we are constantly in the middle of a war.

Weak Christians can't survive in the spiritual battle that is taking place all around them. You have to be ready to stand on the authority and confidence that God has given you. With a strong faith, you can defeat and rebuke Satan when he gets in your face or tries to destroy the people around you.

Lord, I rebuke the devil in your name. I refuse to let him have any room in my life or in lives of any of my friends or family. I will use the power you have given me to bind him. In Jesus' name. Amen.

Extreme Promises

Promises

about

O God, You are my God;
Early will I seek You;
My soul thirsts for You;
My flesh longs for You . . .
Because Your lovingkindness is better than life,
My lips shall praise You.

—PSALM 63:1, 3

For You, Lord, are good, and ready to forgive,
And abundant in mercy to all those who call
    upon You.

—PSALM 86:5

For I am persuaded that neither death nor
life, nor angels nor principalities nor powers, nor
things present nor things to come, nor height nor
depth, nor any other created thing, shall be able
to separate us from the love of God which is in
Christ Jesus our Lord.

—ROMANS 8:38

Beloved, let us love one another, for love is of
God; and everyone who loves is born of God and
knows God. He who does not love does not know
God, for God is love.

—1 JOHN 4:7–8

TRUST THAT
God's Love
Is Constant

Most things in this life don't last very long, but the one thing we can be sure of is God's love. It will never end. It can't because "God is love" (1 John 4:8)—Love is His very nature! He exists, so He must love. He is a bundle of love, waiting to **engulf** any person who will give their heart to Him. There is nowhere you can go that His love won't find you. No matter how fast you run, His love will run faster.

Stop for a minute to think about how much God loves you. Soak it all in. Let Him wrap you in His love. The moment you do, all of your needs for acceptance, fulfillment, and wholeness will be met.

Lord, I thank you that no matter what I have done, your love embraces me anyway. Thank you for filling me today with the reality of your amazing love. In Jesus' name. Amen.

I have come that they may have life, and that they may have it more abundantly.

—JOHN 10:10

For if by the one man's offense death reigned through the one, much more those who receive abundance of grace and of the gift of righteousness will reign in life through the One, Jesus Christ.

—ROMANS 5:17

Yet in all these things we are more than con-querors through Him who loved us.

—ROMANS 8:37

Fight the good fight of faith, lay hold on eter-nal life, to which you were also called and have confessed the good confession in the presence of many witnesses.

—1 TIMOTHY 6:12

For whatever is born of God overcomes the world. And this is the victory that has overcome the world—our faith. Who is he who overcomes the world, but he who believes that Jesus is the Son of God?

—1 JOHN 5:4–5

TRUST THAT
God Enables You to Live
Victoriously

Our God is a champion. He is Almighty God, Creator the universe, and He always wins. Jesus says, "I have overcome the world" (John 16:33). God can never be beaten.

God wants His children to be champions as well. Paul says, "If God is for us, who can be against us?" (Rom. 8:31). Paul took courage from God and confidently said, "I can do all things through Christ who strengthens me" (Phil. 4:13). God wants to breathe the **spirit of a champion** into you today. He designed you to win when you follow Him with all of your heart. Let Him lift you up and make you strong in whatever circumstances you are facing today.

Lord, I thank you that because you are a champion, you made me one too. I don't care what my circumstances are or what people are saying about me. I thank you that you believe in me and that you are making me strong today. In Jesus' name. Amen.

Then God said, "Let Us make man in Our image, according to Our likeness; let them have dominion over the fish of the sea, over the birds of the air, and over the cattle, over all the earth and over every creeping thing that creeps on the earth."

—GENESIS 1:26

For He spoke and it was done; He commanded, and it stood fast.

—PSALM 33:9

Behold, I am the LORD, the God of all flesh. Is there anything too hard for Me?

—JEREMIAH 32:27

And we know that all things work together for good to those who love God, to those who are the called according to His purpose.

—ROMANS 8:28

Eye has not seen, nor ear heard,
Nor have entered into the heart of man
The things which God has prepared for those
    who love Him.

—1 CORINTHIANS 2:9

TRUST THAT
God Is
in Control

One of the most common questions that Christians ask is, "If God is really in control, then **why** do all these bad things happen? **Why** are people starving? **Why** are so many horrible crimes committed?"

After God created the world, He put man in charge of it. But when Adam and Eve gave in to sin, they turned over the world to Satan. In a very real way, Satan rules the earth today, but the Bible says that you are a slave to whomever you obey (Rom. 6:16). So, ask yourself, *Do I obey God or Satan?*

God is only in control of *those who want Him to be in control.* When you invite Jesus to be the center of your life, then you have to submit to Him each day. When you do, He will work things out for your good. He will protect you from the enemy by giving you His power.

Lord, please take control of my life because I know that with you in charge, everything will turn out for my good. I know that I am called according to your will, and I want to obey you. In Jesus' name. Amen.

I have called you by your name;
You are Mine.

—ISAIAH 43:1

Let the wicked forsake his way,
And the unrighteous man his thoughts;
Let him return to the LORD,
And He will have mercy on him;
And to our God,
For He will abundantly pardon.

—ISAIAH 55:7

To him the doorkeeper opens, and the sheep
hear his voice; and he calls his own sheep by
name and leads them out. And when he brings out
his own sheep, he goes before them; and the
sheep follow him, for they know his voice.

—JOHN 10:3–4

You were bought at a price; do not become
slaves of men.

—1 CORINTHIANS 7:23

TRUST THAT
God Wants You to Belong to Him

God made you out of a little bit of Himself. As a result, He cares for you like a father cares for his child. He is constantly **drawn to you,** no matter what you have done or what you have said, no matter how many times you have blown it or how many times you have run from Him. He desperately wants you to belong to Him and be connected to Him so that He can bless your life.

In the same way that a mother hen instinctively watches over her chicks or the way a mother bear protects her cubs, our God instinctively longs to protect us and watch over us. But you only get His care and protection if you stop and turn around—and let Him catch you.

Lord, I thank you that I am not walking around aimlessly and that I was created in your image. Today, I let you catch me once again. I don't belong to this world, I don't belong to peer pressure, and I don't belong to sin. I choose to lay down my life and belong to you. In Jesus' name. Amen.

I love the LORD, because He has heard
My voice and my supplications.
Because He has inclined His ear to me,
Therefore I will call upon Him as long as I live.

—PSALM 116:1–2

For your Father knows the things you have
need of before you ask Him.

—MATTHEW 6:8

But seek first the kingdom of God and His
righteousness, and all these things shall be added
to you.

—MATTHEW 6:33

All things that the Father has are Mine.
Therefore I said that He will take of Mine and
declare it to you. . . . And in that day you will
ask Me nothing. Most assuredly, I say to you,
whatever you ask the Father in My name He will
give you. Until now you have asked nothing in
My name. Ask, and you will receive, that your
joy may be full.

—JOHN 16:15, 23–24

TRUST THAT
God Will Meet
Your Needs

Our God knows our needs even before we ask for them, yet He still wants us **to ask.** He wants us to come to Him because he longs to take care of us.

He understands what we need better than we do. Instead of giving us the things that the world says we need, He will supply what He *knows* we need. When you pray for something that's in God's will, you are releasing His power to do what He already wants to do for you anyway. He will supply our heart's desire if we honestly seek Him.

Lord, I thank you that my life is more than the things I eat and the things I wear. Thank you for supplying all my needs as I continue to seek you with all my heart. In Jesus' name. Amen.

For the Lord God is a sun and shield;
The Lord will give grace and glory;
No good thing will He withhold
From those who walk uprightly.

—Psalm 84:11

For all things are for your sakes, that grace, having spread through the many, may cause thanksgiving to abound to the glory of God.

—2 Corinthians 4:15

Having predestined us to adoption as sons by Jesus Christ to Himself, according to the good pleasure of His will, to the praise of the glory of His grace, by which He has made us accepted in the Beloved. In Him we have redemption through His blood, the forgiveness of sins, according to the riches of His grace.

—Ephesians 1:5–7

Let us therefore come boldly to the throne of grace, that we may obtain mercy and find grace to help in time of need.

—Hebrews 4:16

TRUST THAT
God Will Give You Grace

Grace is simply God's favor toward you. In other words, because God really, really, really, really likes you, He pays special attention to you and treats you with great kindness. Even though you did nothing to earn God's grace, He gives it to you unconditionally, and because you didn't earn it, there is nothing you can do to cause it to go away.

Grace is like a **waterfall of forgiveness** that we must step under each day. That waterfall cleanses us and purifies our hearts. No matter what, you can't stop the waterfall of His grace. Step under it today. Let Him wash you with His care. He will prepare you to live for Him with a pure heart.

Lord, I thank you for your grace and your constant forgiveness. I ask for your waterfall of grace to cleanse me and prepare me to live for you today. In Jesus' name. Amen.

But the Helper, the Holy Spirit, whom the Father will send in My name, He will teach you all things, and bring to your remembrance all things that I said to you.

—John 14:26

Now hope does not disappoint, because the love of God has been poured out in our hearts by the Holy Spirit who was given to us.

—Romans 5:5

But you shall receive power when the Holy Spirit has come upon you; and you shall be witnesses to Me in Jerusalem, and in all Judea and Samaria, and to the end of the earth.

—Acts 1:8

I say then: Walk in the Spirit, and you shall not fulfill the lust of the flesh. For the flesh lusts against the Spirit, and the Spirit against the flesh; and these are contrary to one another, so that you do not do the things that you wish.

—Galatians 5:16–17

TRUST THAT
God Will Give You His
Holy Spirit

You know the Father, and you know His Son, Jesus, but do you know the Holy Spirit, God's helper? The Holy Spirit is the **invisible agent** of God. It is the part of God that works in our hearts to change us and fill us.

When we give our lives to Jesus, He sends His Holy Spirit into our hearts. When we ask God to soften someone else's heart, He sends His Holy Spirit. Jesus promised that after He left the earth, the Holy Spirit would come to us and would be with us always. The Spirit helps us and gives us God's power.

Lord, I thank you for your Holy Spirit. Fill me with the Spirit, and give me power over every temptation that I will face today. In Jesus' name. Amen.

Extreme Promises about

Spiritual Growth

But the hour is coming, and now is, when the true worshipers will worship the Father in spirit and truth; for the Father is seeking such to worship Him.

—JOHN 4:23

For this reason we also, since the day we heard it, do not cease to pray for you, and to ask that you may be filled with the knowledge of His will in all wisdom and spiritual understanding; that you may walk worthy of the Lord, fully pleasing Him, being fruitful in every good work and increasing in the knowledge of God.

—COLOSSIANS 1:9–10

Without faith it is impossible to please Him, for he who comes to God must believe that He is, and that He is a rewarder of those who diligently seek Him.

—HEBREWS 11:6

You are worthy, O Lord,
To receive glory and honor and power;
For You created all things,
And by Your will they exist and were created.

—REVELATION 4:11

HOW TO

Please God

When your first priority is pleasing God instead of yourself or others, then you know that you have reached a deeper level of faith. As children of God, we know that we have matured in our faith when we want to give joy to our Father, when our desire is to **bring a smile** to the face of the living God. Wow, what an honor that is!

Today, do not live to please your friends or even your family; instead, live to please the audience of One, the God of the universe.

Lord, my desire is to bring a smile to your face today. I commit to live and act in a way that shows that I am growing up in you and, as a result, pleasing you. In Jesus' name. Amen.

For this reason I bow my knees to the Father of our Lord Jesus Christ, from whom the whole family in heaven and earth is named, that He would grant you, according to the riches of His glory, to be strengthened with might through His Spirit in the inner man, that Christ may dwell in your hearts through faith; that you, being rooted and grounded in love, may be able to comprehend with all the saints what is the width and length and depth and height—to know the love of Christ which passes knowledge; that you may be filled with all the fullness of God.

—Ephesians 3:14–19

Therefore, laying aside all malice, all deceit, hypocrisy, envy, and all evil speaking, as newborn babes, desire the pure milk of the word, that you may grow thereby, if indeed you have tasted that the Lord is gracious.

—1 Peter 1:25

Grow in the grace and knowledge of our Lord and Savior Jesus Christ. To Him be the glory both now and forever. Amen.

—2 Peter 3:18

HOW TO
Grow in the Spirit

When we are first born again, God gives us brand-new hearts, and we become His brand-new children. It's important that we immediately begin to grow in our faith. Too many people sit in church for years and never grow; they are still just **spiritual babes.** In other words, they still make all kinds of sinful mistakes because they are young in their faith.

Like babies that depend on their parents for food, we need to be fed by our spiritual leaders for a time, but we also need to learn to feed ourselves. We need to read and study the Bible for ourselves, and we need to spend time in prayer with God alone. Open your Bible today and ask God, "Lord please feed me today. I want to grow up, and I need spiritual nutrition to do that."

Lord, I thank you for helping me grow today. I refuse to remain a spiritual baby for the rest of my life. As I read your Word, give me the spiritual nutrition I need to grow in the things of God. In Jesus' name. Amen.

Thanks be to God for His indescribable gift!

—2 CORINTHIANS 9:15

Blessed be the God and Father of our Lord Jesus Christ, who has blessed us with every spiritual blessing in the heavenly places in Christ, just as He chose us in Him before the foundation of the world, that we should be holy and without blame before Him in love.

—EPHESIANS 1:3–4

Giving thanks always for all things to God the Father in the name of our Lord Jesus Christ.

—EPHESIANS 5:20

Every good gift and every perfect gift is from above, and comes down from the Father of lights, with whom there is no variation or shadow of turning. Of His own will He brought us forth by the word of truth, that we might be a kind of first-fruits of His creatures.

—JAMES 1:17–18

HOW TO
Count Your Blessings

A sign of spiritual maturity is choosing to look at the positive instead of the negative. It's choosing to thank God for all the good things that He has given you.

You can count your blessings, or you can focus on what's wrong in your life. What you choose to look at influences your attitude. Concentrating on the negative turns you into a sourpuss, and you end up assuming that you are doomed to have a lousy day. But when you are counting your blessings, you feel lifted up and encouraged—you feel like a winner.

Small children only look at their immediate needs. They are constantly crying out for attention. But mature children of God see the glass as **half full** instead of **half empty,** and they realize that God has given them a lot to be thankful for.

Lord Jesus, today I choose to focus on what you have blessed me with rather than what my needs are. I choose to have a grateful heart. In your name. Amen.

159

I will bless the LORD at all times;
His praise shall continually be in my mouth.

—PSALM 34:1

Oh, clap your hands, all you peoples!
Shout to God with the voice of triumph!
For the LORD Most High is awesome;
He is a great King over all the earth.
Sing praises to God, sing praises!
Sing praises to our King, sing praises!

—PSALM 47:1–2, 6

Because Your lovingkindness is better than life,
My lips shall praise You.
Thus I will bless You while I live;
I will lift up my hands in Your name.

—PSALM 63:3–4

Therefore by Him let us continually offer the
sacrifice of praise to God, that is, the fruit of our
lips, giving thanks to His name.

—HEBREWS 13:15

HOW TO
Praise God

When you praise God, you welcome His presence. When you thank Him for His blessings, He fills you up in a new and rich way.

Too many people only praise God when they are in church, and they only thank God when they receive some really big blessing. People who are spiritually mature realize that no matter how they are feeling, or what they are thinking, the Almighty God is worthy of our praise and adoration *all the time*. Sometimes we feel like praising Him, and sometimes we don't. But He is always worthy of it because **He is God.**

He doesn't need our praise so that He can remind Himself of how great He is. He wants us to praise Him so that *we can remind ourselves* of how incredible He is. When we recognize that He is the **Lord and King** of the universe, we are worthy to enter His presence.

Lord, today I choose to praise you and acknowledge that you are the King of glory, the great God. There is none that compares with you. No matter what goes on around me, I know that you are worthy of honor and adoration. In Jesus' name. Amen.

Extreme Promises

Promises

Making a Difference

And Saul said to him, "Whose son are you, young man?" So David answered, "I am the son of your servant Jesse the Bethlehemite."

—1 Samuel 17:51, 58
(after David killed Goliath)

As for these four young men, God gave them knowledge and skill in all literature and wisdom; and Daniel had understanding in all visions and dreams.

—Daniel 1:17

Then said I:
"Ah, Lord God!
Behold, I cannot speak, for I am a youth."
But the Lord said to me:
"Do not say, 'I am a youth,'
For you shall go to all to whom I send you,
And whatever I command you, you shall
    speak."

—Jeremiah 1:6–7

Let no one despise your youth, but be an example to the believers in word, in conduct, in love, in spirit, in faith, in purity.

—1 Timothy 4:12

164

God Needs Young People

God wants to use young people. He always has used young people, and He always will.

Many times, when we think that God might want to use us, our first response is, "O but Lord . . . I can't. I am too young." That's exactly what Jeremiah said, but God rebuked him by saying, "Don't you dare say 'I am only a youth.' You must go. You will say what I put on your heart" (paraphrase of Jer. 1: 6–7).

God is not looking for **excuses.** He is looking for young people who are willing to **step out.** He wants to use you in the same way that He used David, Shadrach, Meshach, Abed-Nego, Jeremiah, and thousands of other young people. He wants to use you today to make a huge difference in people's lives. Don't hinder God's plan for you. God is counting on you to stand up and make a difference while you are young.

Lord, I thank you that you want to use me in the same way you used young people in the Bible. I make myself available to you today. In Jesus' name. Amen.

So the Lord said to him, "What is that in your hand?" He said, "A rod." And He said, "Cast it on the ground." So he cast it on the ground, and it became a serpent; and Moses fled from it. Then the Lord said to Moses, "Reach out your hand and take it by the tail" (and he reached out his hand and caught it, and it became a rod in his hand), "that they may believe that the Lord God of their fathers, the God of Abraham, the God of Isaac, and the God of Jacob, has appeared to you."

—Exodus 4:2–5

A man's gift makes room for him,
And brings him before great men.

—Proverbs 18:16

And whatever you do, do it heartily, as to the Lord and not to men.

—Colossians 3:23

If anyone speaks, let him speak as the oracles of God. If anyone ministers, let him do it as with the ability which God supplies, that in all things God may be glorified through Jesus Christ, to whom belong the glory and the dominion forever and ever. Amen.

—1 Peter 4:11

Using Your Gifts for God

You may think God only works through people who are extremely talented or gifted in some area, but the fact is that God can use *anyone* to make an impact in people's lives.

God told Moses to look at the rod in his hand, and then He turned the rod into a snake (Ex. 4:2–5). Like Moses, God can use you in a miraculous way if you will look at what is in your hand. In other words, what talent or skill do you have that God could use?

Don't say, "I am not a preacher. I can't really do anything." God doesn't want a world full of preachers. He just wants you to work for His glory in everything you do. **Can you serve** really well? **Can you love** others real good? Whatever God puts in your hand, use it to make a difference in people's lives.

Lord, though I may not be gifted in many things, I ask you to use what you have given me for your glory. Help me to find a way to make a difference for eternity. In Jesus' name. Amen.

A new commandment I give to you, that you love one another; as I have loved you, that you also love one another.

—John 13:34

Greater love has no one than this, than to lay down one's life for his friends.

—John 15:13

Walk worthy of the calling with which you were called, with all lowliness and gentleness, with longsuffering, bearing with one another in love.

—Ephesians 4:2

Since you have purified your souls in obeying the truth through the Spirit in sincere love of the brethren, love one another fervently with a pure heart.

—1 Peter 1:22

Loving People

When Jesus said "love one another," He wasn't asking us to love the whole world at once. He wants us to love **one to another**. In other words, He wants us to love others, one person at a time.

Sometimes we get so busy trying to love *everybody* that we end up *loving nobody.* When we love everybody, it's like our love spills into the ocean and gets watered down, but when we love one person, it's like putting a drop of it into a small glass of water—where it will make a difference.

I encourage you to find one or two people who need God's love, and then reach out and love them really good! Pray for them before the day starts, and think about how you can encourage them.

Lord, today, show me who needs love, and help me to reach out to them. Let them see your love in me, and as a result, let their lives be changed forever. In Jesus' name. Amen.

He who answers a matter before he hears it,
It is folly and shame to him.

—PROVERBS 18:13

Cease listening to instruction, my son,
And you will stray from the words of
knowledge.

—PROVERBS 19:27

And she had a sister called Mary, who also sat
at Jesus' feet and heard His word.

—LUKE 10:39

So then, my beloved brethren, let every man
be swift to hear, slow to speak, slow to wrath.

—JAMES 1:19

Listening to Others

Listening is one of the best ways to show people that you love them. Think about it. When someone looks into your eyes and focuses on what you are saying, you feel like the most important person in the world. And you can make others feel the same way!

So many people go through life feeling like **nobody listens** to them, but you can make a difference by focusing on what they are saying instead of on what *you* are thinking. Too often, we are busy thinking about ourselves when someone is talking. I encourage you to listen by repeating in your mind what the other person just said.

When you give others your full attention, you show them that you care about them. If people feel like what they are saying is important to you, then they'll **pay attention** to you, and you'll be amazed at how God can use you in their lives.

Lord, I thank you for using me to make a difference by listening. I choose to focus on what other people are saying instead of on my own agenda. In Jesus' name. Amen.

LORD, make me to know my end,
And what is the measure of my days,
That I may know how frail I am.

—PSALM 39:4

Whoever loves instruction loves knowledge,
But he who hates correction is stupid. . . .
The hand of the diligent will rule,
But the lazy man will be put to forced labor.

—PROVERBS 12:1, 24

He who walks with wise men will be wise,
But the companion of fools will be destroyed.

—PROVERBS 13:20

To everything there is a season,
A time for every purpose under heaven:
A time to be born,
And a time to die;
A time to plant,
And a time to pluck what is planted.

—ECCLESIASTES 3:2

Making Every Day Count

Too many people live in the past. They think about what they did or what they wish they would have done. Too many others live in the future. They think about what they can't wait to do or what's going to happen tomorrow.

Right now is the time to make a difference for **the rest of your life.** As you leave your room in the morning, don't say, "Tomorrow I might make a difference" or "Maybe next year I'll start a Bible club at school" or "Maybe someday I will go on a mission trip." There are desperate, hurting people all around you right now, and they are waiting for you to touch them. "Someday" is here!

Right now is the only time you have. David wanted to be reminded of the shortness of his life so that he could focus completely on the present. He said, "LORD, make me to know my end, and what is the measure of my days" (Ps. 39:4). Make every day count for Jesus.

Lord, I refuse to waste my life. I will seize the day today. Help me to use my life to make a difference in this world. In Jesus' name. Amen.

173

You are the light of the world. A city that is set on a hill cannot be hidden. Nor do they light a lamp and put it under a basket, but on a lampstand, and it gives light to all who are in the house. Let your light so shine before men, that they may see your good works and glorify your Father in heaven.

—MATTHEW 5:14–16

How then shall they call on Him in whom they have not believed? And how shall they believe in Him of whom they have not heard? And how shall they hear without a preacher?

—ROMANS 10:14

For all the law is fulfilled in one word, even in this: "You shall love your neighbor as yourself."

—GALATIANS 5:14

Influencing Your World

Jesus called His children the "salt of the earth" and the "light of the world" (Matt. 5:13–14). Jesus was saying that He wants you to do more than just exist. He wants you to make a difference.

We live in a dark world, and we are called **to be the light.** We are called **to be the salt** that flavors everything we do with a little bit of the gospel. Once we realize we are a part of God's purpose, we will touch people's lives as we share His love.

God wants us to influence others, not be influenced by others. Instead of being shaped by the world, He wants us to shape the world. Today, go forth and show the world the love of God.

Lord, I thank you for giving me your light and your love. With these, I can make a huge difference in my world. Let me influence others for you. In Jesus' name. Amen.

175

Go therefore and make disciples of all the
nations, baptizing them in the name of the Father
and of the Son and of the Holy Spirit, teaching
them to observe all things that I have commanded
you; and lo, I am with you always, even to the end
of the age.

—MATTHEW 28:19–20

Go your way; behold, I send you out as lambs
among wolves.

—LUKE 10:3

And so I have made it my aim to preach the
gospel, not where Christ was named, lest I should
build on another man's foundation, but as it is
written:
"To whom He was not announced, they shall
see;
And those who have not heard shall understand."

—ROMANS 16:20

And Barnabas and Saul returned from
Jerusalem when they had fulfilled their ministry,
and they also took with them John whose surname
was Mark.

—ACTS 12:25

Sharing Your Faith

Jesus is in the business of using young **people** to shake nations. Maybe you're nervous about sharing the gospel because you don't know everything about the Lord or the Bible. Jesus said, "I send you out as lambs among wolves" (Luke 10:3). Even though His disciples were **young in their faith** like lambs, He sent them off on short trips to various villages to preach. They had never been to Bible school, but He asked them to tell others about Him.

Perhaps you think you're too young to go on a mission trip, but Jesus used young people in His ministry. Maybe you don't think one or two weeks or a month would really matter, but Jesus thought it did. He sent His disciples out for a couple weeks at a time.

I encourage you to go to the mission field, even if you don't feel "called." God wants to use your youthful zeal and energy. If you go, you will never be the same.

Lord, give me the courage to make a difference while I am young. Lord, use me. I want my energy to count for the kingdom of God. In Jesus' name. Amen.

Extreme Promises about

Eternity

For God so loved the world that He gave His only begotten Son, that whoever believes in Him should not perish but have everlasting life. For God did not send His Son into the world to condemn the world, but that the world through Him might be saved. He who believes in Him is not condemned; but he who does not believe is condemned already, because he has not believed in the name of the only begotten Son of God.

—John 3:16–18

Most assuredly, I say to you, he who hears My word and believes in Him who sent Me has everlasting life, and shall not come into judgment, but has passed from death into life.

—John 5:24

For we know that if our earthly house, this tent, is destroyed, we have a building from God, a house not made with hands, eternal in the heavens.

—2 Corinthians 5:1

And this is the testimony: that God has given us eternal life, and this life is in His Son. He who has the Son has life; he who does not have the Son of God does not have life.

—1 John 5:11–12

Eternal Life

God made us in His image. The Bible says "God is Spirit" (John 4:24), which means that we, too, are spirit beings. Your body is a "tent" that holds your spirit (2 Cor. 5:1). When your body dies, your spirit will live on.

But where will **your spirit** go for eternity? God gives us an incredible opportunity to be with Him in heaven if we commit to Him while we are on this earth. Where we spend eternity is our choice. It is our decision.

God wants us to spend eternity with Him. If you know Jesus as your Savior, then you will live forever with Him in heaven.

Lord, I thank you that my eternal life is in your hands because I have entrusted it to you. I want to live eternally with you because I was created for that purpose. In Jesus' name. Amen.

But God will redeem my soul from the power
    of the grave,
For He shall receive me.

—PSALM 49:15

The fear of the LORD is a fountain of life,
To turn one away from the snares of death. . . .
The wicked is banished in his wickedness,
But the righteous has a refuge in his death.

—PROVERBS 14:27, 32

Jesus said to her, "I am the resurrection and
the life. He who believes in Me, though he may
die, he shall live."

—JOHN 11:25

For to this end Christ died and rose and lived
again, that He might be Lord of both the dead and
the living.

—ROMANS 14:9

And as it is appointed for men to die once, but
after this the judgment.

—HEBREWS 9:27

Death

Here's a tough question to answer: Are you ready to die? When faced with the idea of dying, most people start questioning themselves. They ask: *Did I really live a fulfilling life?* The Bible says that a full life comes from knowing God and Jesus Christ. So, you may want to ask yourself: *Do I really know Jesus? Have I given Him my all?*

Here's another tough question for you: If you knew you would be in eternity tomorrow, how would you live your life today? What would you do differently? Would you reach out to more people? Would you be a little bit kinder? Would you share your faith in Jesus with more people?

No matter how you answer these questions, you can start living fully for God today. Make every day count so that when you go to heaven you will be ready to meet God face-to-face.

Lord, I thank you for preparing a place for me in heaven. Lord, I commit to living each day for you like there is no tomorrow. In Jesus' name. Amen.

The name of the Lord is a strong tower;
The righteous run to it and are safe.

—PROVERBS 18:10

And He said to them, "I saw Satan fall like lightning from heaven."

—LUKE 10:18

And the God of peace will crush Satan under your feet shortly.

—ROMANS 16:20

Therefore submit to God. Resist the devil and he will flee from you. Draw near to God and He will draw near to you. Cleanse your hands, you sinners; and purify your hearts, you double-minded.

—JAMES 4:7–8

Be sober, be vigilant; because your adversary the devil walks about like a roaring lion, seeking whom he may devour. Resist him, steadfast in the faith, knowing that the same sufferings are experienced by your brotherhood in the world.

—1 PETER 5:8–9

Satan

The Bible tells us that Satan was an angel in heaven, but when he tried to rebel against God, God quickly kicked him out of heaven (Is. 14:12–15). Jesus describes it this way: "I saw Satan fall like lightning from heaven" (Luke 10:18). God ended the "war" in heaven with a lightening-quick response.

Today, the devil roams the earth like a lion, looking for lives to destroy. He despises us because we remind him of God. We are made in God's image, and every time he looks at us, it reminds him that he lost the battle.

The good news is that when we give our lives to Jesus, He gives us power over the enemy—power over darkness, over sin, and over temptation. **God gives us authority** over the enemy so that we don't have to live in fear of Satan. When we give our lives to Jesus, we can live with great confidence in our ability to rebuke the devil and keep him away from ourselves and those around us.

Lord, I thank you for giving me power over Satan. I thank you for protecting me from the enemy because you care for me. In Jesus' name. Amen.

If your right eye causes you to sin, pluck it out and cast it from you; for it is more profitable for you that one of your members perish, than for your whole body to be cast into hell.

—MATTHEW 5:29

The Son of Man will send out His angels, and they will gather out of His kingdom all things that offend, and those who practice lawlessness, and will cast them into the furnace of fire. There will be wailing and gnashing of teeth.

—MATTHEW 13:41–42

And these will go away into everlasting punishment, but the righteous into eternal life.

—MATTHEW 25:46

The Lord is not slack concerning His promise, as some count slackness, but is longsuffering toward us, not willing that any should perish but that all should come to repentance.

—2 PETER 3:9

But the cowardly, unbelieving, abominable, murderers, sexually immoral, sorcerers, idolaters, and all liars shall have their part in the lake which burns with fire and brimstone, which is the second death.

—REVELATION 21:8

186

Hell

Have you ever wondered if hell is real? The Bible says that it is, but God never intended for any of His children to go there. Hell was made for Satan and his followers. God wants us to go to heaven, but it's not up to God. We have to decide for ourselves where we want to spend eternity.

In the movies, sometimes we hear this line: "I will see you in hell." Similarly, some rock-and-roll stars sing about hell as a place where they can party with their friends. But you can be sure that there will be *no* partying in hell. In fact, the Bible says it's an "everlasting punishment" (Matt. 25:46).

As Christians, we want to let others know that Jesus wants them to be in heaven with Him forever. We want to **shut the gates of hell** and **open the gates of heaven** for those around us.

Lord, help me to rescue people from hell by reaching out to them and letting them know that you love them. Give me just the right words so they can understand the truth about eternal life. In Jesus' name. Amen.

For as the lightning comes from the east and flashes to the west, so also will the coming of the Son of Man be. . . . Immediately after the tribulation of those days the sun will be darkened, and the moon will not give its light; the stars will fall from heaven, and the powers of the heavens will be shaken. Then the sign of the Son of Man will appear in heaven, and then all the tribes of the earth will mourn, and they will see the Son of Man coming on the clouds of heaven with power and great glory. And He will send His angels with a great sound of a trumpet, and they will gather together His elect from the four winds, from one end of heaven to the other.

—MATTHEW 24:27, 29–31

Let not your heart be troubled; you believe in God, believe also in Me. In My Father's house are many mansions; if it were not so, I would have told you. I go to prepare a place for you. And if I go and prepare a place for you, I will come again and receive you to Myself; that where I am, there you may be also. And where I go you know, and the way you know.

—JOHN 14:1–4

Then we who are alive and remain shall be caught up together with them in the clouds to meet the Lord in the air. And thus we shall always be with the Lord.

—1 THESSALONIANS 4:17

The Return of Christ

Jesus promised that He is coming back for His children, and what an incredible day it will be! The Bible says that we will be "caught up" with Him in the rapture (1 Thess. 4:17).

A lot of people think that they can wait to repent on the day that Jesus comes back, but there won't be time for that. Jesus said it would happen as fast as lightening (Matt. 24:27). We should **live** like He is coming back today but **plan** like He is not coming back for fifty years. In other words, we should live today with such an urgency that we touch the lives of other people, but we should also plan for the long-term by preparing ourselves to be used by Him. If we do this, then when Jesus comes back, He will say, "Well done, good and faithful servant" (Matt. 25:23).

Lord, I thank you that you always keep your promises. I know that you will come back. While I am here, help me to make the biggest difference that I possibly can so that there will be more people ready to meet you when you return. In Jesus' name. Amen.

Jesus said to him, "You shall love the Lord your God with all your heart, with all your soul, and with all your mind."

—MATTHEW 22:37

Jesus answered and said to him, "Most assuredly, I say to you, unless one is born again, he cannot see the kingdom of God."

—JOHN 3:3

For God so loved the world that He gave His only begotten Son, that whoever believes in Him should not perish but have everlasting life.

—JOHN 3:16

If you confess with your mouth the Lord Jesus and believe in your heart that God has raised Him from the dead, you will be saved.

—ROMANS 10:9

God's Plan of Salvation

A lot of people go to church but are not born again because they haven't gotten to know Him personally. Today is the day to get to know God for yourself. If you don't know where you will spend eternity, you can decide right now by praying this prayer.

Lord Jesus, today I give you the deepest part of me, my heart. I hold nothing back, and I ask you to take charge, to be my Lord. I believe you died on the cross for me and rose from the dead for me. I pledge my life to you. Forgive me, Lord, for my sins against you. Please cleanse me. In Jesus' name. Amen.

If you just prayed that prayer for the first time, be sure to talk to someone about it who can help you grow in your faith—your parents, pastor, or youth pastor. Also, find a church where other Christians can support your new faith. What an exciting adventure God has planned for you!

We'd like to know about your decision! Contact us at: Teen Mania Ministries, P.O. Box 2000, Garden Valley, TX 75771, 1-800-299-TEEN www.acquirethefire.com **or** www.teenmania.org

Teen Mania Ministries

Teen Mania Ministries is all about helping young people be extreme for God. Here's what we do:

- **Teen Mania Global Expeditions.** Thousands of young people are changing the world as they travel to 30 different countries for missions trips.
- **Acquire the Fire Youth Conventions.** Teen Mania hosts weekly youth conventions across North America where teens learn about radical Christian living.
- **Acquirethefire.com.** Over nine million people visit our site each month. Young people surf our on-line devotions, chat rooms, and discussion boards.
- **Acquire the Fire Dome Events.** Each year, Teen Mania hosts a dome event that challenges teens in their faith. In 1999 and 2000, over 70,000 teens and leaders attended the events at the Silverdome in Pontiac, Michigan.
- **Acquire the Fire Television Show.** Ron Luce hosts a weekly program for teens that airs on several television outlets, such as the Trinity Broadcasting Network.
- **Teen Mania Honor Academy.** Each year, high school graduates live on the Teen Mania campus in Garden Valley, Texas, for an exciting one-year program on faith, leadership, purpose, vision, integrity, and honor.

President and Founder Ron Luce started Teen Mania Ministries with his wife, Katie, in 1986. He has traveled to more than 50 countries, proclaiming the gospel of Jesus Christ. His dream is to empower young people to take a stand for Christ in their schools and in the world.